A GUIDE TO 150 YE
OF CHICAGO ARCHITECTURE

CHICAGO REVIEW PRESS

CONTENTS

Copyright © by Museum of Science and
Industry, Chicago
All rights reserved
Printed in the United States of America
First Edition

ISBN 0–914091–83–2 cloth
    0–914091–81–6 paper

Typography by Typographics, Chicago

Published by Chicago Review Press, 814 N.
Franklin St., Chicago, Illinois 60610

Cover photo courtesy Skidmore Owings & Merrill

The Prints and Photographs Department of the Chicago Historical Society provided the majority of historic photos for this volume.

ACKNOWLEDGEMENTS

This book, put together in a very short time under conditions that were often far from ideal, owes its existence to the splendid cooperation we received from a number of institutions and individuals. For photos we are especially grateful to Larry Viskochil and his staff in the Prints and Photographs collection of the Chicago Historical Society including Maureen Will, Clarence Clark and Anne Steinfeldt for making available prints from this splendid collection. Paul Glassman in the libraries of the Art Institute of Chicago, Bob Sanders at the Chicago Tribune and Tim Barton and Tim Samuelson at the Chicago Commission on Historic and Architectural Landmarks were also very helpful in obtaining photos.

In addition we received photos from the Lake County Museum, Commonwealth Edison, the Chicago Housing Authority, Zenith Electronics Corp., the Civic Opera Building Management, the University of Chicago Law School, Patrick Shaw and Associates, The United States Gypsum Co. and the Scottsdale Merchants Association, as well as photographs of their own work from dozens of architectural offices in the city. We received timely and invaluable help from Darcy Day, a volunteer at the Chicago Historical Society, and from Monica Nolan and Catherine Weese. The book would have been very different without the enthusiastic reception given it by Curt and Linda Matthews at Chicago Review Press.

Certainly one of the most gratifying aspects of preparing this book was the generous assistance we received from the architectural community of Chicago. The staff of many firms in town were bombarded by requests for photos and information and almost all of them obliged us and did so efficiently and quickly. The offices of Bertrand Goldberg, Skidmore Owings and Merrill and Harry Weese were tremendously helpful in assembling our central section on three masters of modern architecture in Chicago, and we would like to extend special thanks to Mary Woolover at SOM, Catherine Ingraham at Bertrand Goldberg's office and Patricia Wray and Jennifer Ungers Klein at Harry Weese Associates.

ROBERT BRUEGMANN

SABRA CLARK

PAUL FLORIAN

DOUGLAS STOKER

CYNTHIA WEESE

A NOTE FROM THE CURATOR

by Ante Glibota

In the original Paris installation of "150 Years of Chicago Architecture" it took nine different galleries to present this extensive show. Now, as the collection returns from its European odyssey to the Museum of Science and Industry, the intricate network of relationships between styles and schools that the exhibition represents can be seen in one location. The technological virtuosity of Chicago architects will find an appropriate milieu here.

The different faces of the exhibition—historical Chicago, modern Chicago, contemporary Chicago—is reunited into a single portrait of a city with the most important new architecture in the world. And yet, sometimes in order for something to be seen with fresh eyes, it must first become foreign. The exhibition thus returns to the city from which it grew, burnished by its European adventure.

From my position as Director of the Paris Art Center, I first reached out to Chicago because it seemed to me to be the wellspring of American architecture. My ambition was to bring Chicago to Europe as the most American city that could explain, through its architecture and urban planning, something about the meaning of democracy. I have written before of the differences between the European and American space and spirit and how the rapid development of the American city depended on a great openness of space and mind. Thus "Chicago sur Seine" was more than a gallery opening in Paris. The presentation of Chicago as a city of architecture to the people of Paris, La Rochelle, Toulouse, and Zagreb fundamentally changed their view of this Midwestern city. Familiar with New York, but ignorant about Chicago, people who came to the exhibition began to replace their cliches about Chicago with richer perceptions. The European "discovery" of this American city was first a hope when we planned this exhibition and then a reality during its one year of travel.

A NOTE FROM THE CURATOR

In returning the architecture of Chicago, in a state of fresh apperception, to its inhabitants we have fulfilled most of our original intentions: "to make known a city and its architecture, without theoretical pretensions, without exclusiveness, and without any biases except those that were imposed on us." But there were some things we could not do. We could not effectively represent all Chicago architects and the numerous individuals within the major firms. Nor could we completely translate the dynamism of the city in its native land. However, on its own soil, the exhibition broadened its representation to include additional firms and new material that we could not transport economically accross the Atlantic. And we have retained the original organization of the exhibition in its four parts: Chicago I, "Early Chicago"; Chicago II, "the Prairie School and Frank Lloyd Wright"; Chicago III, "Realities," where the influence of Mies van der Rohe and the larger Chicago firms are shown; Chicago IV, "Trends," which documents the work of different architects and different currents.

In spite of its size and coverage of 150 years of architectural history, the exhibition originally was not designed primarily for architects. We have continued to strive for simplification by avoiding technical terms and illustrations in the texts and exhibits—and selecting images that speak for themselves—so that the show may reach other people also.

Chicago changed Europe. But how did Europe change Chicago? In at least one way. Chicago became, during its European stay, a new city of "towers" or, as one critic put it, and city of "tours sauvages." This is a somewhat surprising characterization, since most people are used to thinking of New York as the city of sky-scrapers. But from the Water Tower that survived the great Chicago fire to Louis Sullivan's handsome Auditorium, to the great boxes of Mies van der Rohe and the competitive skyscrapers of Skidmore, Owings & Merrill, to Bertrand Goldberg's curving Marina City and Helmut Jahn's gleaming Xerox building, Chicago was understood to be a city of innovative upward motion. In Chicago, these buildings do not create canyons. Instead they develop in a natural, but curious, relationship to each other. The strength and power of these Chicago sky-scrapers—"promethean" as another critic commented—is perhaps emblematic of the new growth of this great city in the European consciousness.

FOREWORD

by Victor Danilov

In 1983, Americans heard about a stunning exhibition on Chicago architecture presented in Paris. The show was so large that it had to be divided into segments and presented at nine locations. The French public and press were overwhelmed by Chicago's spectacular architectural heritage and contemporary innovations.

The exhibition—titled "150 Years of Chicago Architecture: 1933-1983"—contained more than 6,000 photographs and drawings, 33 architectural models, and remnants of historic Chicago buildings. Its contents ranged from the work of such architectural giants of the past as Louis Sullivan, Frank Lloyd Wright, and Ludwig Mies van der Rohe to the imaginative designs of present-day architects like Walter Netsch, Bertrand Goldberg, Harry Weese and Helmut Jahn.

Le Monde praised the show, saying it featured "super-star architecture," while *Le Matin* extolled the exhibition and Chicago—where "the modern city and 20th century architecture were born." The *International Herald Tribune* said the exhibition shows "a visitor more than he would ever get to see on the spot," and the *Wall Street Journal* stated that even Chicagoans who see the show will "appreciate their city with new eyes."

It was against this background that the Museum of Science and Industry approached Ante Glibota, organizer of the exhibition and director of the Paris Art Center, about having the comprehensive show come to Chicago. Arrangements were made to present the exhibition at the Museum in 1985 after it completed its European tour. The *Chicago Tribune* and Carson Pirie Scott & Co. agreed to be the sponsors.

In planning the Chicago showing, about 25% of the original exhibition was changed through updating and supplementing of the content. New buildings, additional architects, more models and artifacts, building materials, a typical architect's office, educational programs, and a multimedia presentation on Chicago architecture have been added to enhance the exhibition.

This publication was prepared to present an overview of Chicago's architectural achievements and to serve as a guide for those seeing the exhibition in Chicago. The Museum of Science and Industry greatly appreciates the cooperation of Chicago's architectural community in making this guidebook possible.

Victor J. Danilov
President and Director
Museum of Science and Industry

INTRODUCTION

A Guide to 150 Years of Chicago Architecture was commissioned by the Museum of Science and Industry to accompany its expanded presentation of the travelling exhibition, "150 Years of Chicago Architecture," curated by Ante Glibota. Museum president, Victor Danilov, asked Robert Bruegmann, Paul Florian, Douglas Stoker and Cynthia Weese to organize a new publication which would complement the original catalog by expanding for the Chicago audience some of the ideas raised in the first publication.

The structure of the book reflects the museum's intention to accommodate the exhibit material to its regional audience. Because the Chicago public is already familiar with its architecture, the editors have sought to present the landmarks of Chicago architecture in a broader context and in greater detail.

To present the historically important works of Chicago architecture as an integral part of the city which spawned it, Chicago's famous buildings are grouped chronologically by decade in Part One. Within each section a variety of buildings typical of the decade accompany views which show the city at its current stage of development; a single prototypical building is also illustrated and discussed in detail.

To clarify the relationship between contemporary architecture in Chicago and the continuum of Chicago architecture, Part Two examines the work of three architects whose work provided alternatives to the Miesian traditions of the Modern Movement: Bertrand Goldberg, Walter Netsch and Harry Weese. The work and career of each are examined in three articles, each written by a well known architecture critic. These pieces are followed by an afterword by Stanley Tigerman.

To update contemporary work begun or completed since the exhibition's inception, Part Three provides a representative cross-section of buildings by contemporary architects.

In Part Four, maps of the exhibit spaces at the Museum of Science and Industry are provided to orient the visitor.

PANORAMA

Robert Bruegmann and Sabra Clark

The presence of architecture seems to loom larger in Chicago than it does in any other city in America. Should a visitor to the city request the cab driver at the airport to take him to Frank Lloyd Wright's Robie House or Mies van der Rohe's Lake Shore Drive Apartments, there is a very good chance, if the driver understands English, that he would know exactly how to get there. And, even if he might not, in fact, take the shortest, least expensive route, he would no doubt attempt to give the rider his money's worth by pointing out some notable architecture along the way.

Throughout the year the city hums with architectural activities. The excellent tours run by the Chicago Architectural Foundation introduce thousands of people to Chicago's major buildings. Both the Chicago Historical Society and the Art Institute are actively collecting architectural drawings and mounting exhibitions. The Landmarks Preservation Council of Illinois and the Chicago Commission on Historic and Architectural Landmarks keep watch over the city's landmark structures. The city also boasts two major schools of architecture, one at the University of Illinois at Chicago, the other at the Illinois Institute of Technology. Dozens of excellent books on Chicago architects and buildings line the shelves of libraries (See bibliography).

PANORAMA

*Robert Bruegmann is Associate
Professor of architectural history at
the University of Illinois at Chicago.
Sabra Clark is assistant curator of
architectural collections at the Chicago
Historical Society.*

With all this interest and attention one might conclude that Chicago architecture was well-charted territory. In fact, all the books and exhibitions, lectures and tours barely scratch the surface. Most have concentrated on a few important architects and buildings located mostly in the Loop and affluent neighborhoods and suburbs. A simple automobile trip out from the Loop to the far suburbs reveals that great chunks of the cityscape, vast industrial complexes with monumental freight terminals and factory structures, whole neighborhoods filled with solid, interestingly varied houses, long commercial strips lined with plate glass and terra cotta facades, small parks with winding roads and substantial field houses, are mentioned in none of the books, visited on none of the tours.

The city itself remains the richest text in which to read the history of Chicago architecture. Although much has been destroyed, what remains is staggering in its quantity and its diversity. What follows does not pretend to give an definitive account of all this. Instead it is a modest attempt to give some kind of idea, decade by decade, of the appearance of various parts of the city and some of its representative buildings as a kind of rough map to the endlessly fascinating terrain of Chicago architecture.

Water Tower and Pumping station. Exterior looking southeast. Photo by Barnes Crosby, c. 1900. (Photo courtesy of the Chicago Historical Society.) ICHI-05876

The rise of Chicago from a stretch of marshy land smelling of wild onion to a large, prosperous city, the railroad hub of the country and a major agricultural and manufacturing center is one of the great epics of 19th century American urban history. Between 1830 and 1870 the population grew from less than 100 to nearly 300,000. By 1870 Chicago, with its huge Union Stockyards, lumber yards and factories was well on the way to becoming the most important heavy industrial center in the country. The city's new wealth was abundantly reflected in the opulent mansarded and dormered stores and hotels on State Street and the substantial Greek revival and Italianate houses of the wealthy along the major roads leading south from downtown. Almost all of this world has disappeared, however, the victim of the great fire of 1871 and rapid redevelopment.

WATER TOWER

1869. Michigan Avenue at Chicago Ave.
William Boyington, architect.
Ellis Cherborough, engineer.

Looking today a little like a toy castle in the shadow of the John Hancock Building and Water Tower Place on North Michigan Avenue, the Water Tower is one of the very few buildings in the business district and Near North side to escape the fire. It was actually the standpipe used to regulate the pressure of the water pumped from the lake by the pumping house which also still stands across the street. Although Chicago sits on one of the largest reservoirs of fresh water in the world, the process of getting good clean water to the city and removing wastes has been a problem from the earliest days until our own time.

Henry B. Clarke House (Widow Clarke House). 1836. Architect unknown. Originally erected at 18th and Wabash. Now at 1855 S. Indiana Avenue in the Prairie Avenue Historic District. HABS photo c.1935. Chicago's oldest existing building, the Widow Clarke House was built in an area that was then at the extreme outer limits of the city's built-up area. (Photo courtesy of the Art Institute of Chicago.)

Section through Water Tower and Water Works. 1869 engraving from "8th Annual Report of the Board of Public Works." (Photo courtesy of the Chicago Historical Society.) ICHI-05883

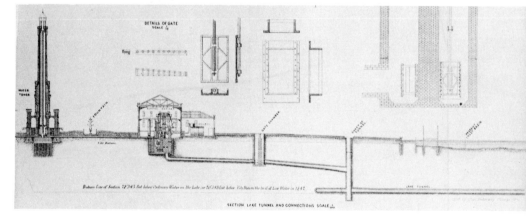

VIEW OF AN ENTIRE BLOCK OF BRICK & STONE BUILDINGS IN CHICAGO ON LAKE ST. BETWEEN CLARK & LASALLE STRS. WHILE BEING RAISED TO THE NEW GRADE A HIGH OF 4 FEET.

Lake Street between Clark and La-Salle showing buildings being raised to new grade. Lithograph published by Edward Mendel, 1860. Until the late 1860s Lake Street was the heart of the business district and boasted four and five story brick and stone buildings. Above the tops of the business buildings could still be seen the masts of the ships docked behind Lake Street and church steeples. (Photo courtesy of the Chicago Historical Society.) ICHI-04307

Michigan Avenue looking north from Congress, pre-fire. Photo c. 1868-69. Visible in this photo are the elegant houses of Michigan Avenue, the via-duct of the Illinois Central Railroad out in the lake and in the distance the great grain elevators at the mouth of the Chicago River looming larger than anything else on the horizon. (Photo courtesy of the Chicago Histor-ical Society.) ICHI-04438

Cook County Courthouse. Northwest corner of Clark and Washington Streets. Architect: John Van Osdel. Erected 1853. Photo by William Shaw, 1858 after alterations and a third story were added. This building was destroyed by the fire of 1871. (Photo courtesy of the Chicago Historical Society.) ICHI-00433

Riverside, Illinois. Plan of town laid out by Olmsted, Vaux and Co., 1869. Riverside, with its curving roads, large houses and ample lots, was one of the most important planned picturesque suburbs in America.

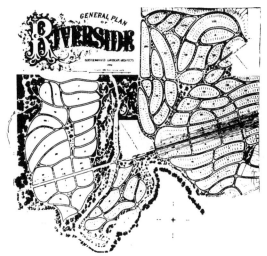

Third Presbyterian Church. Architect unknown. Washington Boulevard and Carpenter Street. 1858. Photo Briggs and Secord. One of the major landmarks of the pre-fire west side. (Photo courtesy of the Chicago Historical Society.) ICHI-14280

Palmer House Exterior. Barnes-Crosby photograph. (Photograph courtesy of the Chicago Historical Society.) ICHI-19225

The great fire of 1871 destroyed nearly $200,000,000 in property including virtually the entire business section. Almost 100,000 people were left homeless. It looked for a short time as if several of Chicago's long-time midwest rivals would pull ahead of it. But within a few weeks reconstruction had begun and by the end of the decade Chicago had roared back into full frenetic activity. By 1880 the city's population had reached over a half million. The business district, now centered on State Street, was thriving and streets full of houses, many of them inexpensive "balloon frame" construction, started to reach out toward the horizon.

Palmer House
1875. Monroe and State Streets.
John Van Osdel.

No institution better symbolized the post-fire era than the opulent Palmer House of 1875. Built at a cost of over $2.5 million to replace a similar building constructed shortly before the fire, its pavilions, dormers and corner turret proclaimed to every passerby its status as Chicago's most prestigious hostelry. The interiors were equally lavish and boasted carloads of marble and imported woods, mosaics, frescoes and other embellishments.

Kitchen at the Palmer House. Print from "The Palmer House Illustrated," 1876. (Photograph courtesy of the Chicago Historical Society.) ICHI-14464

Interior view looking toward the Grand Staircase. Stereoptican photograph. (Photograph courtesy of the Chicago Historical Society.) ICHI-18918

The Palmer House Rotunda. Print from "The Palmer House Illustrated," 1876. (Photograph courtesy of the Chicago Historical Society.) ICHI-14465

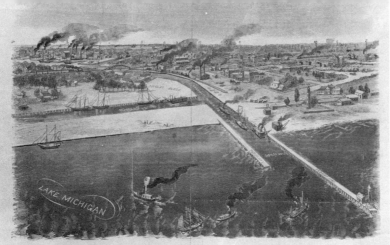

BIRDSEYE VIEW OF SOUTH CHICAGO — CALUMET HARBOR.

"Bird's eye view of South Chicago Harbour," print from Chicago and its Suburbs by Everett Chamberlin, 1874. The Chicago River, the initial reason for the founding of the city, quickly became inadequate to handle the city's shipping needs. Starting in the 1870's the Calumet River on the south side started to develop as an alternate port. Further improvements made the Lake Calumet area one of the country's most important centers for heavy industry. (Photo courtesy of the Chicago Historical Society.)

Clark Street south from Randolph. Photo from stereograph. 1874. This area, destroyed by the fire in 1871, demonstrates the speed with which the city was rebuilt, and the newly installed telephone poles, heavy traffic and abundant signs give some evidence of the enormous energy which made this rebuilding possible. (Photo courtesy of the Chicago Historical Society.) ICHI-04147

Second Presbyterian Church 1872, architect James Renwick. 1836 S. Michigan Avenue photo by Barbara Crane, taken 1975. Renwick was one of the country's best known church architects of the mid-century and this church was one of the most fashionable in the city. After a fire in 1900 another prominent architect, Chicago's Howard Van Doren Shaw, remodeled the church providing a spectacular new interior. (Photo courtesy of the Chicago Commission on Historical and Architectural landmarks.)

Jackson-Thomas House c. 1873. Architect unknown. 7053 N. Ridge. Photo, Bob Thall, 1984. This grand Italianate house was built for one of the founders of the Rogers Park Land Company. It was later occupied by Thomas, an ink company owner. (Photo courtesy of the Chicago Commission on Historical and Architectural Landmarks.)

Interior of Second LaSalle Street Station (Michigan Southern and Lake Shore Railroad Station) 1872 architect W. W. Boyington. Southwest corner of S. LaSalle and W. Van Buren Streets. The Second LaSalle Street Station was constructed after the fire of 1871 destroyed the first structure. The two buildings, both designed by Boyington, were similar in design with limestone facades and towers. This photograph c.1874-79 shows the metal trusses and corrugated iron and glass roof of the train shed. In 1903 a new station was built on this site, but it has been demolished also. (Photograph courtesy of the Chicago Historical Society.) ICHI-05326

Union Stock Yard Gate c.1879. Design attributed to the firm of Burnham and Root, Exchange Avenue at Peoria Street. The Union Stock Yards were established in 1865, originally occupying almost a square mile. Surrounded by the workers homes and isolated from the downtown district, the area became a city in itself. This limestone gate is all that remains today of the yards and stands somewhat incongruously at the entrance to an industrial park on the site of the yards. (Photograph courtesy of the Chicago Historical Society.) ICHI-19107

Interior of the theatre, photo by Richard Nickel c.1968. (Photograph courtesy of the Chicago Commission on Historical and Architectural Landmarks.)

The 1880s were boom years in Chicago. This fact was confirmed by a simple glance at the skyline. In 1880 the tallest buildings in the Loop rose five and six stories. By the end of the decade buildings rising 16 stories towered above their neighbors. People from all over the world came to Chicago to catch a glimpse of the future. Not everyone, even in Chicago, was optimistic about what they saw. Many Chicagoans found the new scale, congestion and pollution oppressive. In increasing numbers they took advantage of new, more efficient means of transportation including the cable car and electric trolley to allow them to move further and further from downtown. Along the great boulevards of the south side stately stone houses appeared. For citizens of more modest means row upon row of cottages went up, and along the rail lines the suburbs grew rapidly. In 1889 Chicago more than trebled in size when it annexed nearby townships, bringing its population to over one million people.

Auditorium Building
1886-89, South Michigan Ave.
and Congress St.
Adler and Sullivan.

Chicago in the 1880s was still in many ways a frontier boomtown. Industry was thriving and the city was growing by leaps and bounds. Many Chicagoans, however, were becoming increasingly embarrassed by the city's reputation as a place lacking cultural amenities and labels like "Porkopolis" used to describe it by citizens of the more established eastern metropolitan areas. The Auditorium Building was the most important attempt in this period to remedy this situation and to create a home for high culture in Chicago. Financed by a group of Chicago's civic leaders, this huge block was to house a auditorium, a hotel and an office building. Restrained on the exterior, the auditorium's interior was elaborately decorated by architect Louis Sullivan. With its swirling floral motifs, lavish use of gold, murals and mosaics, and the soft glow of hundreds of the new electric light bulbs, the auditorium had an astonishing, almost barbaric splendor the equal of anything anywhere else in the country.

Exterior view, showing the Annex across Congress Street, the latter erected 1893 to designs of Clinton D. Warren. (Photograph courtesy of the Chicago Historical Society. ICHI-00575)

Interior of the hotel lobby c.1900. (Photograph courtesy of the Chicago Historical Society. ICHI-00588)

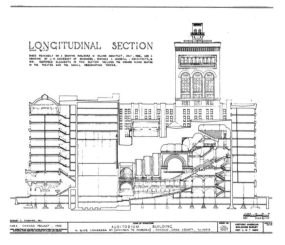

Section drawing 1963 H.A.B.S. Chicago project, showing Wabash Street office building on the right, the Auditorium in the center and the hotel on Michigan on the left.

Interior of the hotel dining hall c.1890. This room now houses the library for Roosevelt University. (Photograph courtesy of the Chicago Historical Society. ICHI-0052)

Interior of the hotel bar c.1890. (Photograph courtesy of the Chicago Commission on Historical and Architectural Landmarks.)

The lakefront looking N. from 35th street, c.1880's. This photograph shows elegant outside residential neighborhoods from the vantage point of the tracks along the lakefront. (Photograph courtesy of the Chicago Historical Society. ICHI-04834)

Cook County Court House and City Hall, completed 1885, block bounded by N. LaSalle, W. Randolph, N. Clark and W. Washington. Architect James J. Egan. Three days after the fire of 1871 authorization was given for the construction of a new court house and city hall to replace the building destroyed in the fire. This ill-fated building took almost twelve years to build, cost over $4 million, and was already too small at the time of its completion. After it was also found to be structurally unsound it was torn down in 1906. (Photograph courtesy of the Chicago Historical Society. ICHI-14388)

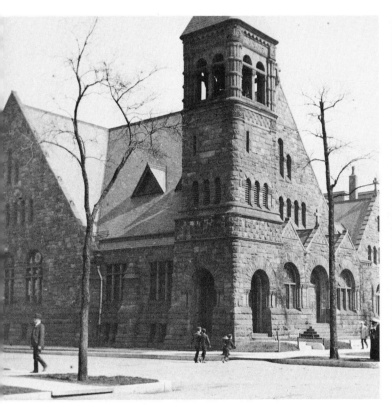

Church of the Epiphany. 1885, 201 S. Ashland Avenue. Architects Burling and Whitehouse. This church is constructed of rusticated sandstone in the Romanesque style made popular by Richardson. Four piers support the ceiling through a system of wooden trusses that meet in a rosette in the center of the church. (Photograph courtesy of the Chicago Historical Society.)

Glessner House 1886. Henry Hobson Richardson 1800 S. Prairie Avenue. The photograph was taken by George Glessner, c.1895. One of a handful of Chicago buildings designed by the great Boston architect, the house was designed with fewer windows on the street but opening up to a courtyard. The style used by Richardson, loosely derived from the Romanesque, was immensely popular in Chicago. (Photograph courtesy of the Chicago Historical Society. ICHI-01197)

Pullman Administration Building, 1880-81. Corner of E. 111th Street, S. Cottage Grove Avenue. Architect Solon S. Beman. Photograph 1908. The Administration Building was at the center of George Pullman's model industrial town. The 4300 acre site also contained the sleeping car plant, homes for the workers, a library, hotel, theatre, school, hospital, market and church. The whole project cost almost $8 million. (Photo courtesy of the Chicago Historical Society. DN-6819)

Pullman houses, c.1881. There were over 1400 housing units, primarily two story brick row houses and some apartment buildings. Although Pullman was perhaps the most perfect factory town ever constructed, its design was not enough to prevent one of the bloodiest strikes in American labor history in 1894. (Photograph courtesy of the Chicago Historical Society.)

Dearborn Station (Polk Street Station) 1883-5. Polk and Dearborn Streets. Architect Cyrus L. W. Eidlitz, photo. 1907-08. The Dearborn Station was considered the most picturesque of Chicago's stations. Later the peaked roofs were removed and the tower truncated. In recent years the shed was removed and the headhouse has languished but current plans call for the re-use of the station. (Photograph courtesy of the Chicago Historical Society.)

Rookery Building, 1885-1888. 209 S. LaSalle Street, architects Burnham and Root. The building took its name from the preceding structure on the site, a water tower that housed a great portion of the city's pigeon population. This photo shows the lobby court, originally an airy space of lacy iron work covered by a skylight. The need for water-proofing destroyed the effect of the skylight and in 1905 the Lobby was remodeled by Frank Lloyd Wright retaining the elegant iron work. The court was at the bottom of the large interior space that afforded light and air to all the offices not facing the street. (Photograph courtesy of the Art Institute of Chicago.)

Randolph Street east from Clark 1889. This photo is probably taken from the Sherman House, a 300 room hotel built in 1872. In the foreground a cable car mingles with horse-cars. (Photograph courtesy of the Chicago Historical Society.)

Transportation Building Doorway.
Architect Louis Sullivan. Photo by
C.D. Arnold. (Photograph courtesy of
the Chicago Historical Society.)
ICHI-02279

The period leading up to the 1893 fair was one of the most active in Chicago's history. The early years of the 1890s saw a frenzy of activity in the Loop, climaxing the boom of the 1880s. The city's first elevated line was constructed to the south side in anticipation of the fair and this in turn helped fuel a boom in apartment construction. Some of Chicago's most important institutions,such as the University of Chicago and the Newberry Library, were founded in this period. Others, like the Art Institute and the Chicago Public Library, built themselves major new buildings. Also in the decade of the 90s Chicago saw to completion one of the largest municipal undertakings in urban history: the Sanitary and Ship Canal reversed the flow of the Chicago River and solved for a time the pressing problems of waste removal.

The World's Columbian Exposition of 1893

If the skyscraper can be seen as the icon of the 1880s, the Court of Honor of the 1892 World's Columbian Exposition might fill this role in the 90s. In contrast to the black city to the north rose the gleaming white city of the fair in Jackson Park. With its harmonious classical architecture and careful planning, the fair provided a lesson in how Chicago might transform itself from a brutal business place into the image of the "City Beautiful." This was the impetus which ultimately led to Daniel Burnham's 1909 Plan of Chicago and to a major series of public works in the 20th century.

Reconstruction of the Fine Arts
Building (now the Museum of Science
and Industry) 1930. View looking
northeast; Graham, Anderson, Probst,
and White architects for reconstruction. Charles Atwood of the D.H.
Burnham Company Architect of
original building.

Interior of the Agricultural Hall.
Architects McKim, Mead and White.
(Photograph courtesy of the Chicago
Historical Society.) ICHI-13682

View of the Wooded Island and Lagoon from the Roof of the Liberal Arts Building. C.D. Arnold photo. ICHI-02539

Court of Honour. Photo by C.D. Arnold. ICHI-02526

Palace of Fine Arts. Architect Charles B. Atwood of the D.H. Burnham Company. (Photograph courtesy of the Chicago Historical Society.) ICHI-02226

Getty Tomb, 1890, Graceland Cemetery, architect Louis Sullivan. Photo 1975 by Barbara Crane. Some of Sullivan's finest ornamental work decorates the Getty Tomb. The lace-like stone top is balanced by the plain lower half. The intricate bronze work of the doors elaborates on the stone motif. (Photograph courtesy of the Chicago Commission on Historical and Architectural Landmarks.)

Dearborn Street looking north from Congress Street c.1899 photo by Barnes and Crosby. On the far right stands the Como Building, (1887) designed by John Van Osdel, a center for printers and publishers and the Manhattan Building (1890), next door, by W. L. Jenney, the first 16 story building in America. Continuing to the left are the Plymouth (1899) designed by Simeon B. Eisendrath, the Old Colony (1894) by Holabird and Roche, and the Fisher (1896) by D. H. Burnham and Company. (BC-298)

Brewster Apartments, Atrium, 1893, 2800 North Pine Grove. Architect Enoch Hill Turnock. Photo 1982 by Bob Thall. This view of the skylit atrium reveals the elaborate grill work of the stairway and elevator. (Photograph courtesy of the Chicago Commission on Historical and Architectural Landmarks).

Washington Park Club House c.1891, Cottage Grove Avenue between 61st and 63rd Streets, architect Solon S. Beman. This club, formed in the 1880s, was not only a major social gathering place but it was host to the American Derby which advertised one of the largest purses in the country. (Photograph courtesy of the Chicago Historical Society.) ICHI-03630

Art Institute of Chicago, 1892, South Michigan Avenue and East Adams Street, architects Shepley, Rutan and Coolidge. This grand neo-classical design forms the core of today's vast complex. For the Art Institute and Chicago Public Library of the same years, Chicagoans went to the Boston architecture firm that succeeded H.H. Richardson for designs. (Photograph courtesy of the Chicago Historical Society.) ICHI-00889

Erecting Lake Street Elevated Line, on Market near Madison, c.1892. The Lake Street el was one of the first lines to be constructed. Small steam trains were used until 1897. Eventually the el was extended to most parts of the city and some suburban areas. (Photograph courtesy of the Chicago Historical Society.) ICHI-05371

Dining room. (Photograph courtesy of the Chicago Commission on Historical and Architectural Landmarks.)

By 1910 the city's population had risen to over two million. Although it would eventually reach over three and a half million during World War II, the era of enormous population growth was over for the central city. The new growth was at the periphery of the city and in the suburbs. This was made possible by the rapidly expanding transportation system, notably the efficient elevated trains which had first appeared in the 1890s. The early years of the century also saw the appearance of a new wave of classicism in office buildings, producing massive, monumental structures in the Loop and a new, midwestern kind of residential architecture which has been called the Prairie House.

The Robie House
1909, 5757 South Woodlawn Avenue.
Frank Lloyd Wright

The Robie House is the most famous example of Frank Lloyd Wright's domestic work of the first decade of the 20th century, the period in which he created a startlingly new form for the American dwelling, the Prairie House. With its severely abstract horizontal lines, wide overhanging roof and long, attenuated shape, it must have startled the residents of Hyde Park when it went up in 1909-10. It is still surprising after 75 years.

The Plan of the Ground Floor and
Main Floor, drawings from
Ausgefuhrte Bauten und Entwurfe,
published by Frank Lloyd Wright,
Germany, 1910.

Exterior, photo by Richard Nickel.
(Photograph courtesy of the Chicago
Commission of Historical and Archi-
tectural Landmarks.)

Window detail, H.A.B.S. photo by
Cervin Robinson, 1963. (Photograph
courtesy of the Chicago Commission
on Historical and Architectural
Landmarks.)

Hull House complex, 800 block South
Halsted Street. Opened by Jane
Addams in 1899, Hull House quickly
became a major social force in one of
Chicago's most distressed neighbor-
hoods. The majority of the buildings
were erected to the designs of Irving
K. Pond and his brother Allen in the
first decade of the 20th century.
(Photograph courtesy of the Chicago
Historical Society.) ICHI-19228

Holy Trinity Russian Church (now Cathedral) and Rectory, 1903, 1121 North Leavitt Street, architect Louis H. Sullivan, photo, Charles R. Clark, 1906. Here Louis Sullivan drew on Russian Provincial style architecture to meet the tastes of the church's congregation. Ornamentation is restrained on the exterior but lavish on the interior. (Photograph courtesy of the Chicago Historical Society.)

Orchestra Hall (Theodore Thomas Orchestra Hall), 1905, 220 South Michigan, architects Burnham and Company. Ninth floor by Howard Van Doren Shaw (1908) photo 1977 by Barbara Crane. This elegant brick and limestone classical revival structure has been the home of the Chicago symphony since 1904 when it left Sullivan's Auditorium Theater. In this building the auditorium is at the rear and rises four stories. (Photograph courtesy of the Chicago Commission on Historical and Architectural Landmarks).

Artesian Avenue. This c.1900 photo is labeled "East side of Fairview North from Weston". The house going up on the right shows clearly the balloon frame construction that was a major factor in Chicago's rapid growth. (Photograph courtesy of the Chicago Historical Society.) ICHI-00076.

Marshall Field and Company, 1892-1907, D.H. Burnham and Company, State and Washington Streets. The earliest surviving portion of the store is the 1892 portion in the right, at the corner of Wabash and Washington. The State Street portion of the store was erected in two parts, the northern half in 1902 and the southern in 1907. One of Chicago's grandest classical structures, Field's appearance suggests its owners were building for the ages. (Photograph courtesy of the Art Institute of Chicago.)

State Street looking north from Madison, photo c.1905. In this view the heavy post-fire buildings to the right and the Columbus Memorial Building of 1893 stand in sharp contrast to the austere classical Marshall Field store further north. Only the first half of the State Street front was completed by the time of this photo.

Chapin and Gore Building, 1904, 63 East Adams, Richard E. Schmidt, architect. This modest commercial building sports one of the most personal and intriguing facades in the Loop. (Photograph courtesy of the Chicago Commission on Historical and Architectural Landmarks.)

Outer lobby to cooperative apartments.
Color photo by Kathleen Collins,
1980-81. (Photograph courtesy of the
Chicago Historical Society.)
ICHI-18918

The 1910s were marked by a great war, a post-war depression, and the city's first major race riots, but they also witnessed substantial building downtown and major work on the roadways, parks and bridges proposed by Daniel Burnham in his 1909 *Plan of Chicago*. The completion of the Michigan Avenue Bridge in 1920 opened North Michigan Avenue and the near north side to intensive development. Work on Grant Park was pushed forward and the Field Museum constructed at its southern border.

1550 N. State Parkway
1911-12. Marshall and Fox.

Usually considered the most elegant apartment building in Chicago, 1550 N. State Parkway was designed by Benjamin Marshall of the firm of Marshall and Fox, the city's premier creators of hotels and apartment buildings for the affluent. With its suave, Parisian-inspired facade, enormous and lavishly appointed apartments, and location overlooking Lincoln Park, the building has housed some of Chicago's most prominent families.

Plan of ground floor, 1911.

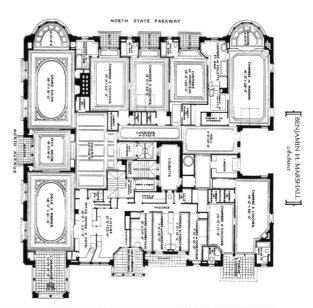

Exterior view. (Photograph courtesy of
the Chicago Historical Society.)
ICHI-17843

Carl Schurz High School, Milwaukee Avenue and Addison Street, 1908-10. Dwight H. Perkins. One of the largest and most impressive structures by a "Prairie School" architect. (Photograph courtesy of the Commission on Historical and Architectural Landmarks.

New Market Square, Lake Forest, Howard Van Doren Shaw, architect, 1916-17. Photo 1917, Charles Hull Ewing Photo Collection, CHS. An early planned shopping center, New Market Square was built across from the railroad station as the centerpiece of Lake Forest's downtown. Shaw ingeniously adapted his design from the architecture of European villages to give the ensemble a domestic scale consistent with the houses he was creating for some of Chicago's wealthiest citizens. (Photograph courtesy of the Chicago Historical Society.) ICHI-18923

Michigan Avenue looking north from Balbo, Barnes-Crosby photo c. 1915. The opulent Blackstone Hotel by Marshall and Fox, 1909, dominates this portion of Michigan Avenue which was largely filled in during the first decade of the 20th century. (Photograph courtesy of the Chicago Historical Society.) ICHI-19153

First Congregational Church of Austin, 5701 W. Midway Park, 1905, architect William Drummond. Photo from Western Architect, 1915. Designed by one of Frank Lloyd Wright's disciples, this modest church has a monumentality much greater than its small size would suggest was possible.

Waiting room at Christmas. (Photograph courtesy of Chicago Historical Society.) ICHI-18925

The Chicago area boomed in the 1920s. A new crop of dramatic skyscrapers loomed above older buildings in the Loop after height limits were revised in the 1923 zoning law. This law permitted higher buildings if they stepped back as they rose. Architects responded by creating mountain-like towers increasingly stripped of ornament and soaring up to the clouds. At the same time, mile after mile of new housing was constructed, and the suburbs expanded dramatically. Prosperity brought home ownership into reach for more and more families and the automobile made the new suburban developments accessible. Even larger buildings in the Loop and more extensive suburban subdivisions were on the drawing board at the time of the Stock Market crash of 1929.

Union Station

1916-25, Jackson Blvd., Adams, Canal and Clinton Streets.
Graham, Burnham and Co.
and Graham, Anderson, Probst, and White successively.

The railroads were largely responsible for Chicago's enormous development in the late 19th century, but they also created vast planning problems for the 20th century. Dozens of lines came into Chicago from all directions, crossing and re-crossing each other and arriving at stations located all around the periphery of the Loop. Union Station was the most ambitious attempt to date to try to rationalize and consolidate this vast, unwieldy system. The station, constructed 1916-1925 to designs of Graham, Burnham and Co. (later Graham, Anderson, Probst and White) consisted of two main parts, a large waiting room in an office building to the west and, to the east, between Canal Street and the River, the Concourse. Unfortunately the spectacular concourse is gone, demolished in 1969.

View of concourse interior. Photo: Chicago Burlington & Quincy Rail-road Co. (Photograph courtesy of the Chicago Historical Society.) ICHI-05328

Union Station, exterior view from southeast showing concourse in fore-ground and main building behind. Photo c. 1925. (Photograph courtesy of the Chicago Historical Society.) ICHI-05319

Union Station under construction, Photo: Daily News, 1924. (Photograph courtesy of the Chicago Historical Society.) DN 77-361

The Tivoli Theater, 1921 Cottage Grove and 63rd Streets, Rapp and Rapp, architects, photo 1927. The Tivoli was one of many elegant movie palaces scattered around the city. Its owners, Balaban and Katz, often combined musical productions and contests featuring the cinema stars. The Tivoli, seating over 4,000, was one of Chicago's largest theaters and served the booming Woodlawn commercial strip. (Photograph courtesy of the Chicago Historical Society.) ICHI-01771

Marshall Field Garden Apartments, 1929-30. Sedgwick Street, Evergreen Avenue, Hudson Avenue, and Blackhawk Avenue, architects Andrew J. Thomas and Ernest R. Graham. This was the largest philanthropic housing development of its day and considered one of the most handsome. Developed by the Estate of Marshall Field, the purpose was to provide moderate-priced apartments close to the downtown area. There were 628 units ranging from $35 for a three-and-one-half-room unit to $63 for a six-room apartment. (Photograph courtesy of the Chicago Historical Society.) ICHI-18921

Civic Opera House, 1928-29. Graham, Probst and White. Wacker Drive between Madison and Washington. View of lobby. The Civic Opera Building was a fitting successor to Adler and Sullivan's Auditorium. A huge structure, it contained offices, the hall for grand opera, the smaller Civic Theater, and some of the most sumptuous interiors in Chicago. (Photograph courtesy of the Opera Building Management.)

Michigan Avenue looking north, 1925. Photo by Kaufmann and Fabry. The Tribune Tower (Hood and Howells, 1923-25) and the Wrigley Building (Graham, Anderson, Probst and White, 1919-21, 1924) dominate this 1920s photo of Michigan Avenue. They were among the first structures to go up after the completion of the Michigan Avenue Bridge, which transformed residential Pine Street into the commercial boulevard called North Michigan Avenue. (Photograph courtesy of the Chicago Historical Society.) ICHI-18515

Aerial Skyline view looking north, 1929. In the foreground Grant Park Stadium (Soldier Field, Holabird and Root, 1923-25) can be seen, and north of it the Field Museum (D.H. Burnham and Co. and Graham, Burnham and Co., 1911-20) and Shedd Aquarium (Graham, Anderson, Probst and White, 1928-29).

Construction of Wacker Drive and Jeweler's (Pure Oil) Building, c. 1926, photo by Raymond Trowbridge. The two-level drive, envisioned in Burnham's Chicago Plan of 1909, displaced, along with other riverside real estate, the South Water Street Market. The upper level was designed for city traffic and the lower road for heavy commercial use. The Jeweler's building, along with the nearby Wrigley, form one of the most extensive displays of terra cotta in the city. (Photograph courtesy of the Chicago Historical Society.)

Straightening the Chicago River, 1929. Photo from the Daily News. One of the civic improvement projects realized under the direction of the Chicago Plan Commission and its director Charles Wacker was the straightening of a bend in the Chicago River between 12th and 18th Streets. The project, recommended in the Burnham Plan of 1909 and undertaken with the hope of improving congested traffic on both land and water, was completed in 1930. (Photograph courtesy of the Chicago Historical Society.) DN 89,537

Chicago Board of Trade Building, Jackson Street at the head of LaSalle. Holabird and Root, 1928-30. View of lobby. Barbara Crane photograph, 1974. With its metal, glass and marble, the lobby of the Board of Trade is one of the sleekest interiors of the 1920s anywhere. Expertly executed and dramatically lit, this space was the last word in up-to-date styling. (Photograph courtesy of the Chicago Commission on Historical and Architectural Landmarks.)

Aerial view of Blue Island, Illinois, 1924 photo by Kaufmann & Fabry Company. Founded with heady expectations, Blue Island was overshadowed by the commercial success of its thriving neighbor, Chicago, but it did become an important manufacturing center. (Photograph courtesy of the Chicago Historical Society.) ICHI-18922

Skyride, designed by bridge engineers
David B. Steinman and Holton D.
Robinson. (Photograph courtesy of the
Chicago Historical Society.)

As the Great Depression deepened in the 1930s, construction in the metropolitan area came to a near standstill. Even major architectural firms dropped to a handful of employees as the total amount of construction plummeted to levels lower than at any time since the Civil War. Besides a few suburban houses, most of the building projects that were carried out involved governmental public works including roadways, post offices and housing projects. In Chicago the emergence of new, avant garde architectural ideas from Europe was symbolized by the arrival in the city of Mies van der Rohe in the late 1930s.

1933 Century of Progress Exposition

One of the few bright spots in the otherwise grim 1930s was the 1933 fair. Planned by a group of Chicago businessmen in the late 1920s, the fair was designed by some of the best known Chicago architects of the day, including John Holabird, Edward H. Bennett and Hubert Burnham, as well as by major architects from elsewhere, notably Raymond Hood, Harvey Wiley Corbett, Paul Cret and Arthur Brown. Brilliantly colored, innovative in materials and design, the fair buildings created a strikingly festive stageset for Chicago's biggest celebration of the 1930s.

Travel and Transportation Building,
Edward Bennett, John Holabird and
Hubert Burnham. Kaufman and Fabry
photograph. (Photograph courtesy of
the Chicago Historical Society.)
ICHI-17408

House of Tomorrow, architect George
Fred Keck, Hedrich-Blessing photo-
graph. (Photograph courtesy of the
Chicago Historical Society.)

Aerial view of the Fair looking south
from the Skyride. (Photograph
courtesy of the Chicago Historical
Society.) ICHI-18920

Avenue of Flags. (Photograph courtesy of the Chicago Historical Society.)

Dedication of Lake Shore Drive Bridge, 1937. The design for the bridge to link Lake Shore's South and North Outer Drives was approved in 1927. Because of funding problems the project was not finished until 1937 with the total cost for the segment from Ohio to Monroe reaching $11,500,000. This photograph was taken during the ceremony in which President Roosevelt dedicated the bridge on October 5, 1937. (Photograph courtesy of the *Chicago Tribune*.)

Benjamin J. Cahn House, 1937, 270
South Western Avenue, Lake Forest.
Architects George Fred Keck and
William Keck. The Cahn House,
intended to be a weekend retreat,
contrasted dramatically with the
traditional image of a Lake Forest
house both in its forms and bright wall
colors. Photo by Hedrich-Blessing.

Adler Planetarium, 1930, 900 E.
Achsah Bond Drive, architect Ernest
A. Grunsfeld, photo c. 1933. This
early planetarium building is covered
in polished red and black granite.
The cylindrical planetarium chamber
at the center of the building reaches
to a dome 68 ft. high. (Photograph
courtesy of the Chicago Commission
on Historical and Architectural
Landmarks.)

Lake County Tuberculosis Sanatorium, 1939, Belvedere Road, Waukegan, Illinois, architects William Pereira, Ganster and Henninghausen. Appropriately for a sanitorium, the balconies were cantilevered well out into the fresh air and the detailing, clearly based on contemporary European architects such as the great Finnish architect Alvar Aalto, recalls nautical structures. (Photograph courtesy of the Lake County Museum.)

Esquire Theater, 1938, 58 E. Oak Street, architects William and Hal Pereira, photo 1983 by Bob Thall. The Esquire Theater was one of the first motion picture theaters to depart from the traditional movie house styles. Pereira subsequently left Chicago to found a very successful practice in Los Angeles. (Photograph courtesy of the Chicago Commission on Historical and Architectural Landmarks.)

Lobby, 1951 photo by Hedrich-
Blessing.

Because of World War II the first half of the 1940s saw very little except war-related construction. After the armistice pent-up demand was enormous, but it took several years for the economy and the building industry to gear up for large scale new construction. The result was that Chicago looked much the same in 1950 as it had in 1930. This was a condition that would soon change dramatically.

860-880 Lake Shore Drive
1949-51, Ludwig Mies van der Rohe.

Put up immediately after World War II, in 1948-51, these buildings probably more than any others heralded post-war modern architecture. Designed by Mies van der Rohe, the extreme simplicity of form and straightforward use of steel and glass contrasted dramatically with the pre-war buildings to each side. These two identical towers, set at right angles to one another, have become the prototype for hundreds of similar structures but hardly ever have these later buildings been marked by the same care and attention to detail as is seen here. Looking at them today, it is hard to believe they are nearly 40 years old.

Exterior, from the lake, c.1958, photo by Arthur Siegel. (Photograph courtesy of the Chicago Historical Society.) ICHI-17859

Apartment interior, 1951 photo by Hedrich-Blessing.

View of apartments under construction. 1950 photo by Hedrich-Blessing.

Ida B. Wells Public Housing Project (aerial view), 1937-41, King Drive, Cottage Grove, 37th, 39th Streets, architect Alfred Shaw. This is one of four housing projects built in Chicago before World War II, this one by the newly founded Chicago Housing Authority rather than the Federal Government. In the post-war years this kind of prototype was abandoned for such projects and highrise construction became the rule. (Photograph courtesy of the Chicago Housing Authority.)

Jeffery Avenue, south of 76th Street, 1947 photo by Otho B. Turbyfill. The post-war housing shortage was met in part by simple austere apartment complexes like this one. (Photograph courtesy of the Chicago Historical Society.) ICHI-01355

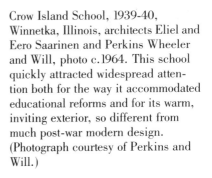

Crow Island School, 1939-40, Winnetka, Illinois, architects Eliel and Eero Saarinen and Perkins Wheeler and Will, photo c.1964. This school quickly attracted widespread attention both for the way it accommodated educational reforms and for its warm, inviting exterior, so different from much post-war modern design. (Photograph courtesy of Perkins and Will.)

Florsheim Factory, 1946, Canal and Adams Streets, architect Alfred Shaw of Shaw Metz Dolio. The continuous strip windows in this early post-war building announced the new steel and glass architecture of the post-war years. (Photograph courtesy of Patrick Shaw and Associates.)

View of entrance area. Ezra Stoller
photograph. (Photograph courtesy of
Skidmore Owings Merrill.)

By 1950 the stage was set for a radical transformation in the city. Downtown large new office buildings went up for the first time since the Depression. A massive road building program was set in motion in an attempt to relieve traffic congestion. Superhighways, several with new mass transit lines running down their median strips, radiated out from the Loop. Slum clearance and rebuilding changed large areas adjacent to the Loop, while suburban expansion exploded out into the hinterlands. The 1950s marked a decisive turning point in architectural style as the unornamented steel and glass box downtown replaced the stepped back stripped classical skyscraper and the post-war split level and ranch house in the suburbs replaced the period revival house.

Inland Steel Building
1957, 30 N. Monroe,
Skidmore Owings Merrill
(Bruce Graham, designer in charge.)

It was not until the mid-1950s that office building construction resumed on a big scale. Of all the early post-war office structures perhaps the most elegant was the 19-story headquarters of the Inland Steel Co. by Skidmore, Owings and Merrill. By placing the columns on the exterior of the building and the elevators and other services in their own enclosure outside the office area, they created large column-free glass-clad office spaces that when stacked created a striking arrangement of horizontal floor levels and vertical exterior columns. The use of blue-green glass and stainless steel gave the whole a brilliant jewel-like quality.

Plan of typical floor.

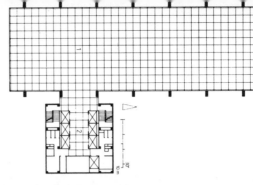

Exterior from west. Hedrich-Blessing
photograph. (Photograph courtesy of
Skidmore Owings Merrill.)

Exterior from southwest. Hedrich-
Blessing photograph, 1957.

International Minerals and Chemical Corporation Administration and Research Center, Perkins and Will, architects and engineers, Skokie, Illinois, 1958. Two suburban office structures provide 158,100 sq. ft. for an Administration and Research Center on a 23 acre site in suburban Skokie. An adaptation of the European modernist "international style", the complex forms a grid, from the placement of the two buildings to the geometrical shape of the reflecting pool and the contrasting black and white exterior panels. Photograph by Hedrich-Blessing. (Photograph courtesy of Perkins and Will.)

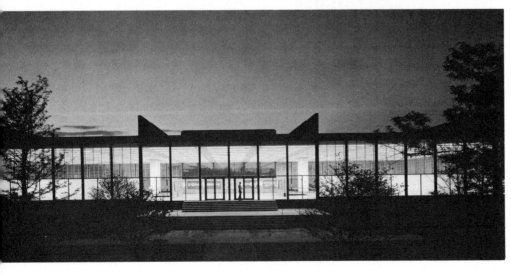

Crown Hall, Illinois Institute of Technology, State Street at 34th, 1955-56, Ludwig Mies van der Rohe and Pace Associates, architects. IIT's Chicago campus expansion of the early postwar years was unparalleled among privately endowed universities. Built to house the Institute's Departments of Architecture Planning and Design, Crown Hall's main level is a single 120 x 220 x 18 ft. space enclosed by glass and steel. The completely open space was made possible by a roof suspended from four exposed rigid frames. Photography by Hedrich-Blessing.

Lake Meadows Apartments, 1950-60, architects Skidmore Owings Merrill. Lake Meadows is located between King Drive and Cottage Grove Avenue, 31st to 35th Streets. One of the largest post-war redevelopment projects, the Lake Meadows housing development consisted of 10 buildings containing 2033 units on 100 acres. It was developed by the New York Life Insurance Company as a racially integrated housing for middle and upper income families. Photograph by Howard N. Kaplan, HNK Architectural Photography. (Photograph courtesy of Skidmore Owings Merrill.)

Prudential Building, 1955, East Randolph and Stetson Streets. Architects, Naess and Murphy. The Prudential Building was the first major tall office building in Chicago since the 1930s. In many ways it still follows in its general lines the model of Rockefeller Center and other pre-war buildings. (Photograph courtesy of Murphy/Jahn.)

Blast Furnace and Ore Docks, Gary, Indiana, photo c.1950. The city of Gary, Indiana is the result of the U.S. Steel's decision to build a modern plant complex on the undeveloped shore of Lake Michigan where the intersection of lake, river and railroads offered ready access to raw materials and markets. Gary, named for Elbert A. Gary, the Chairman of the Board of the Corporation, was an instant city. Five months after its incorporation in July of 1906, it had 10,000 inhabitants. Increasing demands for steel throughout the country made Gary the largest city in the metropolitan area of Chicago.

Home in Beverly Park District, photograph 1952. In the 1950s, growth of automobile ownership, the construction of new roads and a rapidly expanding economy made possible a suburban housing boom. The ranch and split level houses were developed as a response to the new, fast-paced and servantless middle class living. (Photograph courtesy of the Chicago Historical Society.) ICHI-18276

Aerial view from northwest with Loop
in background. (Photograph courtesy
of Murphy/Jahn.)

The post-war building boom continued through the 1960s, surpassing in dollar value construction in any previous decade. But at the same time vast areas of the city slid further into decline. This process was greatly accelerated by racial tensions and the riots of the late 1960s. As the city tried to deal with its problems the suburbs continued to boom. In fact at some point during this decade the balance of population shifted from the city to the adjacent suburbs. As this occurred regional shopping centers, corporate offices and industrial parks drew business and jobs away from the Loop, making the suburbs less dependent on the city. Some urban experts went so far as to predict the city was doomed, that it would be replaced by developments along the interstate roads.

O'Hare Airport
1959-62, Naess and Murphy,
C.F. Murphy and Associates and Others.

By the 1950s Midway Airport on Chicago's south side, already the world's busiest, was clearly inadequate for the great jet boom that was in the offing. Land for the new airport, on the northwest side, had been purchased in 1946. Construction began in 1959 to the designs of Chicago architects Naess and Murphy. Finished in 1962, the airport's original terminals were set on the perimeter of a polygonal central space that was mostly occupied by parking. The airport has become the center of an extensively developed area of office buildings, industrial parks and hotels. Although there have been numerous suggestions that Chicago needs a third, even larger, airport, for the moment it is hoped that a major expansion at O'Hare will meet increased demand.

View of Control Tower (I.M. Pei and
Associates) with Terminal II in back-
ground. (Photograph courtesy of
Murphy/Jahn.)

Aerial view. (Photograph courtesy of
Murphy/Jahn.)

University of Chicago Law School, 1958-60, Eero Saarinen, architect. A complex lining the Midway Plaisance, consisting of a black glass clad library, a low classroom wing and an auditorium structure. The buildings enclose a courtyard with pool, fountains and a sculpture by Antoine Pevsner. (Photograph courtesy of the University of Chicago Law School.)

John Hancock Center, 1969, 875 North Michigan. Architects Skidmore Owings and Merrill (Bruce Graham, design partner; Fazlur Kahn, senior project engineer). One hundred stories high, clad in black anodized aluminum and tinted glass and enlivened by the great crossed steel braces, the Hancock Building is the colossus of North Michigan Avenue. A city unto itself, the complex contains commercial spaces on floors 1-5, parking for 1200 cars on floors 13-41, and the apartments from floors 44-93. The observatory, restaurants and bar occupy 94-96. Photograph by Hedrich-Blessing. (Photograph courtesy of Skidmore Owings and Merrill.)

Dresden Nuclear Power Station Unit 1, 1960. General Electric Company and Bechtel Corporation. This, the first nuclear power station in the state, was built on the outskirts of Chicago. With its 11 nuclear plants Illinois has the largest number of any state in the country. (Photograph courtesy of Commonwealth Edison.)

Richard J. Daley Center (originally Chicago Civic Center), 1965. Block bounded by Washington, Randolph, Dearborn and Clark Streets. C.F. Murphy Associates supervision architects (Jacques Brownson, chief architect) with Skidmore, Owings and Merrill, and Loebl, Schlossman, Bennett and Dart associates, architects. A civic office and courtroom building with unusually large structural bays, clad in Corten self-weathering steel. The plaza to the south of the building opens the facade of the city-county building to the west and was the first in a series of plazas which opened Dearborn Street during the sixties. (Photograph courtesy of Murphy/Jahn.)

United Air Lines Education and Training Center, 1960-70, Elk Grove, Illinois. Architects Skidmore Owings and Merrill (senior designer Myron Goldsmith; partner in charge Bruce J. Graham). The buildings are situated on a landscaped park overlooking a lake. The administration building is a 700 ft. long two-story structure connected with a two-story training center. The administration building contains three interior courts for natural lighting. Photograph by Ezra Stoller. (Photograph courtesy of Skidmore Owings and Merrill.)

Carl Sandburg Village, 1963-68, Division, LaSalle, Clark and North. Solomon, Cordwell, Buenz and Associates. One of the city's most conspicuous examples of "urban renewal." Parking is underground. The deck above, slightly raised above city sidewalks, serves as a more private entry to a variety of low rise housing and apartment towers. (Photograph courtesy of Solomon Cordwell Buenz & Associates.)

View into atrium of shopping area.
(Photograph courtesy of Loebl
Schlossman Hackl.)

Although population and jobs continued to flow out of Chicago throughout the 1970s, there were abundant signs of new life. As the city started to re-orient its economy from heavy industry toward service-related business, new construction was spurred in the Loop. Giants like the Standard Oil and Sears buildings were erected. Neighborhoods like Lincoln Park and Old Town saw a new influx of affluent citizens, often, however, replacing existing, less affluent citizens. As the decade progressed the minimal modern style of the post-war era came under increasing attack. Keystones and entablatures made a reappearance along with pastel shades and eye-catching curves and diagonals. According to some observers Chicago was entering the "post-modern" era.

Water Tower Place

*1976, Michigan Avenue, Chestnut,
Seneca and Pearson Streets.
Loebl Schlossman Bennett and Dart,
with C.F. Murphy and Associates and
Warren Platner for the interior spaces.*

Water Tower Place represents a new generation of urban mixed use spaces. Drawing on the experience of nearby Marina City with its apartments and commercial spaces, and on the great suburban regional shopping centers such as Woodfield Mall, Water Tower Place consists of a 12-story shopping center, theater, office spaces, luxury hotel and condominiums. The building was commissioned by the Urban Investment and Development Co.

View of Ritz Hotel lobby. (Photograph courtesy of Loebl Schlossman Hackl.)

Elevation along Pearson Street showing parking, shopping area, offices, hotel and condominiums. (Photograph courtesy Loebl Schlossman Hackl.)

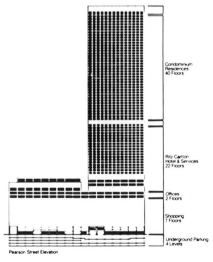

View of exterior from southeast. (Photograph courtesy Loebl Schlossman and Hackl.)

View of Loop from southeast, 1972.
Photograph by Jerry Tomaselli,
Chicago Tribune. This view shows
construction on two of Chicago's
tallest structures: the Sears Tower and
the Standard Oil Building, 1974.
(Photograph courtesy of the *Chicago
Tribune*.)

Baxter Laboratories, Central Facilities
Building, 1975,
Deerfield, Illinois. Architects
Skidmore Owings Merrill. The out-
standing feature of this building is
the structural system in which two
columns support the cable suspension
roof. The 288 ft. wall of glass that
covers the side of the building faces a
lake and landscaped park. Photograph 1977 by Howard N. Kaplan.
(Photograph courtesy of Skidmore
Owings Merrill.)

The Portals, 1971, Grant Place at Sedwick, Booth and Nagle, James Nagle designer. Low-scale and brick-walled, this set of 50 duplex apartments indicates the increasing attention architects in the 1970s started to pay to surrounding, older buildings. (Photograph courtesy of Nagle Hartry and Associates.)

4A Equipment Building and Tower, Northbrook, Gerald Horn of Holabird and Root, architects. Designed by a firm that produced hundreds of telephone buildings over many decades, this building celebrates new technology by its minimal forms, and careful steel and glass detailing. Hedrich-Blessing photograph. (Photograph courtesy of Holabird & Root.)

Arco Station, 1972-73, Route 83 and Rand Road, Mount Prospect, Booth and Nagle, architects, Larry Booth, designer. This station was intended as a prototype for a new generation of service station based on minimal services and minimum prices. It has since been demolished. (Photograph courtesy of Booth Hansen & Associates.)

Woodfield Mall, aerial view, 1971, Jickling & Lyman architects. The world's largest enclosed mall at the time of completion, Woodfield Mall opened with three full-line department stores and over 2,000,000 square feet of space under roof. (Photograph courtesy of the *Chicago Tribune*.)

Plan of typical floor. Photo by Keith
Palmer and James Steinkamp.

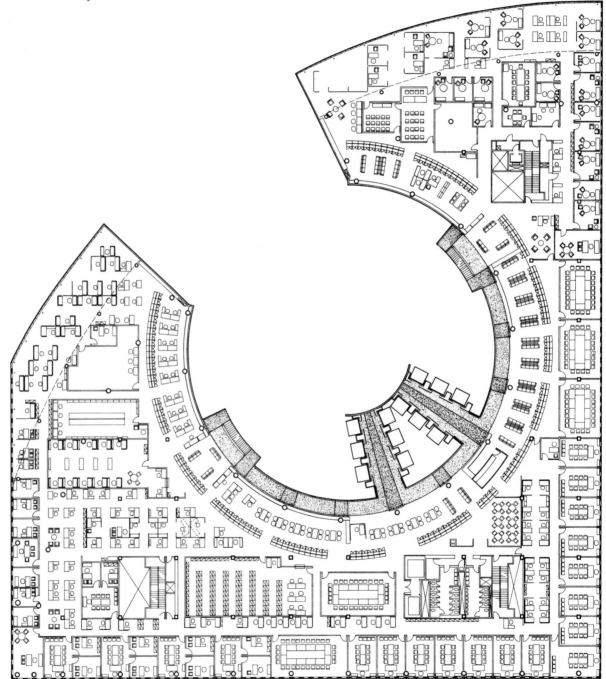

Despite the unrest of the 1960s, the energy crisis of the 70s, an out-migration to the sunbelt, and an invasion of competing foreign goods, Chicago has not only survived but in some ways is more vibrant than ever. Construction in the loop and North Michigan Avenue continues. The near south, west and north sides are turning into extraordinarily lively mixed residential and commercial areas. Although a drive through town reveals boarded-up buildings and abandonment as well as vast areas of aging housing, it also reveals lots of recent repair work and freshpaint. The suburbs, no longer mere bedroom communities, are coming of age as fully developed places for living, working and recreation. The Chicago area in the 1980s is just what it has been for over a century: a gigantic, vastly complicated organism, American's great inland city, the metropolis of the midwest and home of some of the world's most interesting architecture.

State of Illinois Building
1985, Helmut Jahn, Murphy/Jahn, Inc.

Easily the most controversial structure in the city in decades, the State of Illinois may end up the most controversial building in Chicago ever. The building is about as different as it could be from its governmental neighbors, the severe City-County Building by Holabird and Roche, 1905-12 and the powerful Richard J. Daley Center designed under the supervision of Jacques Brownson of C.F. Murphy Assoc. and built 1963-66. Time will tell whether this design is a flash-in-the-pan or a portent of things to come in Chicago architecture.

View of the atrium. Photo by Keith Palmer and James Steinkamp.

View of exterior from the northeast. Photo by Keith Palmer and James Steinkamp.

Cumberland Station, CTA O'Hare line, 1983, Perkins and Will. The extension of the Milwaukee line to O'Hare Airport was one of the major new public works projects of recent years. Included in the project were several new stations including this one that

gives access to a rapidly growing office and commercial district near the airport. Photograph by Howard N. Kaplan. (Photograph courtesy of Perkins and Will.)

333 West Wacker Drive office building, 1983. Kohn Pederson Fox architects, Perkins and Will associate architects. Faced with one of the most conspicuous sites in Chicago, the architects took full advantage of the river frontage by creating a curved facade of green glass that echoes the shape of the bend and reflects the river and surrounding structures. (Photograph courtesy of Perkins and Will.)

American Academy of Pediatrics, Elk Grove Village, 1985, Hammond Beeby and Babka, Inc. For a suburban site near the airport expressway this building was meant to be an updated version of a classical villa. The body of the building was clad in two colors of brick. The entry porch, major garden front colonnade and pediment were executed in painted steel. (Photograph courtesy of Hammond Beeby and Babka.)

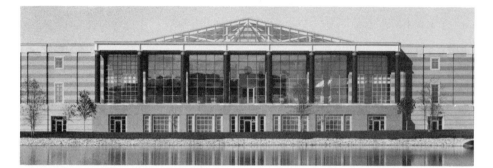

Anti-Cruelty Society Addition, 1977-81, LaSalle Street at Grand Avenue, Stanley Tigerman, architect. The high false-front gable, aluminum siding and comic cut-out windows were used to give the institution a friendly image. Literal historical elements like the gable are hallmarks of what has been called the "postmodern" style and Stanley Tigerman has been one of its most vocal proponents. (Photograph courtesy Tigerman Fugman McCurry.)

One Magnificent Mile, 1980-83, Michigan Avenue and Oak Street, Skidmore Owings Merrill; Senior design partner Bruce J. Graham. The faceted shape of One Magnificent Mile is created by three hexagonal, reinforced concrete tubes that end at varying heights. The building has been designed for a variety of uses. The first three floors contain commercial space and restaurants. Office space reaches from the 4th to the 19th floor. Above are 181 condominium units including a swimming pool, club, outdoor terraces. Hedrich-Blessing photograph. (Photograph courtesy of Skidmore Owings Merrill.)

Mergenthaler loft condominiums, renovation 531 South Plymouth Court, 1980, Kenneth Schroeder Associates, architects. A linotype building converted into 21 loft condominiums. This building was one of the first major examples of a significant trend in Chicago area construction in which commercial buildings are being

remodeled into stylish homes for a new generation of affluent white-collar city dwellers. In this case the shell of a small restaurant was left standing in front of the building as a sculptural object. Photograph by Ron Gordon. (Photograph courtesy of Kenneth Schroeder.)

Chestnut Place, Weese Hickey Weese architects, 1982, State Street at Chestnut. View of lobby with murals by Richard Haas. Where earlier generations of architects had marbles and other fine materials at their disposal; many contemporary architects find themselves limited by budget to plaster board and paint. Here trompe l'oeil specialist Haas took his inspiration from the medieval Florentine church of San Miniato in Florence. Paul Zakoian photograph. (Photograph courtesy of Weese Hickey Weese.)

MASTERS

This section examines in some detail the careers of three important masters of modern architecture in Chicago. Although they constitute no "school" of architecture and have produced distinctive works quite different from one another, they do share certain characteristics. One is that the three men were each born in Chicago, Goldberg in 1913, Weese in 1915, and Netsch in 1920. Each was raised in the area, but went out of town to school, Goldberg first at Harvard and then at the Bauhaus in Germany, Weese at MIT and Cranbrook and Netsch at MIT. Each returned to Chicago to practice, starting his career just before or after the Second World War. Goldberg set up his own firm in 1937. Weese opened his in 1941. Netsch never practiced on his own but he developed a considerable autonomy within the structure of the giant Skidmore Owings Merrill organization.

More important than these biographical similarities, however, are basic assumptions about architecture and about life which the three men seem to share. Each can be called a modern architect in the full sense of that word. Each believes that the architect plays an enormously important role in human society and is perhaps the figure best equipped to decide what the built environment ought to look like. Each has an essentially optimistic attitude about technology, believing that it is still important to pursue all kinds of structural ideas, new building materials, computer use and other technological ideas. Finally, each of the three seems to support the proposition that architecture is a rational pursuit. Although initiation or whimsy can play a part, ultimately decisions must be based on something much more solid that mere individual preferences.

In the end, the three have found themselves throughout their careers somewhat at a distance from what the journals have labeled the "mainstream." Although they shared many of the ideas of other modernists, their own buildings looked quite different from the Miesian designs that were thought to be "mainstream" Chicago modern architecture. They have also kept their distance from a new generation of Chicago architects who have rejected many of the basic assumptions on which their own work rests, and whose work often appears to them capricious and arbitrary.

The articles that follow, each commissioned from a distinguished writer on architecture, explore some of these themes. In his postscript, Stanley Tigerman, speaking for the "post-modern" generation, discusses the influence of the three on younger architects.

BERTRAND GOLDBERG

by Allan Temko

Chicago's finest poets have been architects. To purify the language of building has been the chief aim of the Chicago School through its several phases, from the romantic visions of Louis Sullivan and Frank Lloyd Wright to the classic idealism of Mies van der Rohe and his followers. Philosophically, in quite different ways, the most profound Chicagoans have all drawn organic truths from nature, but they have always expressed them in the syntax of industrial technology. It is this shared approach to structure and mechanical systems, as the basis of a new architectural art, that unites the rather special figure of Bertrand Goldberg—Chicago's great poet of urban community—with the city's other masters.

Yet he stands apart as vividly as the circular grace of Marina City against the adjacent rectangular block of Mies' IBM building. The contest goes beyond the obvious differences between the plastic freedom of concrete, Goldberg's preferred material, and the strict Miesian discipline of steel. Whereas the black office building stands aloof in the city, complete in itself as a statement of abstract corporate strength, Goldberg's elating cylindrical towers are vitally lodged in the surrounding urban fabric. Nonetheless they, too, soar by themselves in the skyline, as tall buildings should in Chicago.

When completed in 1962, they were in fact the tallest structures of reinforced concrete in the world; at 684 feet, they still rank among the highest, and to see them erected at the start of the 1960s was a remarkable demonstration of Goldberg's inventiveness.

The round utility cores went up first, supporting themselves as they ascended, lifting so slenderly that they swayed visibly in wind. People wondered if they were unstable, but they were uncommonly strong and efficient. As an architect who is also an excellent engineer, Goldberg had seen the possibility of using "slip-form" construction on an unprecedented scale: a system in which the cores acted virtually as their own cranes, and then remained as armatures to which the rest of the buildings were attached, like petals to the centers of flowers.

The floral pattern of the 900 apartments—450 in each tower—was thus a high tech metaphor of nature. The floor plans resemble nothing so much as daisies, extending from dense centers to the curving tips of the open balconies which give Marina City such a wonderful mood of diversity, of liberating choices, within a consistent, repetitive organic order.

That diversity is the key to democratic life in huge industrial cities, Goldberg never doubted. Compared to the coercive pigeon-holing of the inmates of Le Corbusier's Unite d'Habitation in Marseilles, France (at the time, the most famous residential megastructure of the modern movement), Marina City— with twice as many residents—is festive and free, especially in fine weather when secretaries and executives, lawyers and school teachers, are out on balconies, enjoying cookouts and views of the loop and the lake. But its urban meanings go much deeper. The topmost forty stories spiral downward through seventeen levels of parking to a multi-use horizontal base, which is the key to the civic design. An elevator ride links the lofty apartments to the shops, restaurants, ice rink, and health club far below, beside the river, where boats sail out from the community's own marina, which gives this city-within-a-city its name.

Marina City, done when Goldberg was in his late forties, is the fulcrum of his career, just as River City—the serpentine mixed-use complex under construction along the riverbank south of the loop— will probably be its culmination. Between these two great projects he has designed housing, office buildings, cultural facilities, schools, and especially hospitals and medical centers, in which his concept of community steadily evolved while he further explored the expressive qualities of rational building systems.

If none of the grand designs, not even Marina City or River City, had ever been carried out quite as he wished, enough has been realized—in projects on paper as well as in finished buildings—to constitute a nearly all-inclusive city of the mind. Unlike an Internationalist "Radiant City," set on a Utopian *tabula rasa*, it is not a universal prescription for human behavior, but rather a large set of economic and social opportunities, ever widening in response to scientific and cultural changes, which were playfully described in an article on his innovative hospital designs as "Goldberg's variations."

Although Goldberg has built convincingly in places as different as Tacoma and Phoenix, Milwaukee and Mobile, his imagined city could not be every city, certainly not San Francisco delicately arrayed on its hills, still less an ancient capital so laden with history as Paris or Rome.

But it is quintessential Chicago, supreme industrial metropolis, an invented fact, stretching mile upon mile back from the lake across the featureless plain. A useful way to consider Goldberg's work, indeed, is to think of him literally as an inventor. In certain ways he recalls Buckminster Fuller, who was struggling in Chicago—his chosen base for remaking the world in a machine-image—when Goldberg returned in 1933, at the age of twenty after college at Harvard, the old Cambridge School of Architecture (which preceded the Graduate School of Design), and then a stint at the doomed Bauhaus and in Mies' office in Berlin.

Back home, Goldberg inevitably designed his own airflow automobile in 1936, but with four wheels, three years after Fuller produced his three-wheeled Dymaxion car. Following Fuller's lead again, he experimented in 1938 with cable-hung roofs: the Clark Street gas station suspended from two masts, so that traffic could pass unimpeded under the canopy, and more adventurous than charming, the transparently enclosed North Pole ice cream stand in River Forest, a "building on wheels" which could be "dismounted and moved to any location" if anyone wanted to, because all the single-masted portable building needed was "electricity, water, and a sewer connection." These early works, combining science, industry and aesthetics, were in the high Bauhaus tradition, but with very American verve and wit. Many inventions followed, particularly in prefabricated housing during World War II. Others included: a mobile penicillin laboratory for the OSS; plywood and plastic freight cars (sabotaged by a dog-in-the-manger steel industry even during a severe war time shortage of rolling stock); and after the war, mass-produced bathrooms and prefabbed house kitchens. These last failed to become assembly-line prototypes because of the confusion and backwardness of building codes.

But Goldberg as an inventor was always primarily an architect, concerned not merely with technology but with the art of building and its impact on man. To this logical structural designer, the creation of space was inseparable from its psychological meaning.

One exceptional opportunity to plumb the problem of space came when flamboyant film producer Mike Todd (the rather mad creator of "Smellorama") asked him to do a radically new kind of movie house. The result was the Cinestage Theatre in Chicago in 1956, in which Goldberg devised a dematerialized presence for images and sounds in space, without a traditional stage or any frame at all for the movie screen. This went far beyond Gropius' "total theatre." It was altogether "live theatre," a forerunner of more advanced cinema technologies. The experience, if not the actual details of the design, had a pivotal effect on Goldberg's later work. It was not coincidental either that an artist such as Albers, one of Goldberg's favorite teachers, was brought in as a master of light and shadow to do the entrance, and that Goldberg himself devised the ceiling lighting of lucite rods.

What Goldberg hoped to impart was a cultural intensity which rudimentary functionalists had tried to iron out of architecture. A sense of immediacy, of fine art in the midst of daily life, was indispensable to a new concept of community.

Few modern architects, especially in America, possessed the broad refinement of Bertrand Goldberg. His grandfather arrived in Chicago before the Fire of 1871, and in 1913 saw his grandson born into a cultivated Jewish patriciate which prized music, the fine arts, literature, and philosophy, together with sound business sense. It was natural for the young man to go east to a Harvard still partly under the spell of Santayana and Whitehead, where a platonic sense of beauty somehow entered the interrelationship of science and the modern world. Later he spent time in Germany, although it was becoming dangerous even for a foreign Jew to study there, not to speak of appreciating the sardonic theatre of Brecht and

Marina City, 300 North State Street, Chicago, Illinois, 1963. Photo by Hedrich-Blessing.

The round utility cores Marina City under construction, 1959. Photo by Portland Cement.

North Pole Mobile Ice Cream Store, River Forest, Illinois, 1938. Photo by Hedrich-Blessing.

Weill. In the strange hiatus between the dying of the Weimar Republic and the brutal rise of the Nazi dictatorship, Goldberg humorously regarded Mies as "God the Father," and tried to understand "not only what he said, but what he didn't say." Mies' enigmatic quotations from St. Augustine and St. Thomas Aquinas, or Spinoza, alone were not enough for the American midwesterner.

There was also the raw, uninhibited energy of Chicago itself, a huge machine of a city from the heroic age of smoke and steel, with an unsurpassed capacity to build. Goldberg, although he knew it would have to become a different, smokeless city, responded to the city's enormous technological power. One of his goals was "simple industrialization." In designing a steel-framed garage, he made a list of all the steel sizes necessary for the job and was "shocked to discover how many different steel sizes and dimensions were required by a small, single-story building." This realization made Goldberg question whether there was a design solution in which uniform dimensions could be used for columns and beams. There was: he substituted a circular plan for a rectangular one. In 1957 an unbuilt motel design for Phillips Petroleum, called "Motel 66," called for two circular towers on a rectangular base—not much different, although far smaller, than the configuration of Marina City which would be designed two years later in 1959 and which would serve as a point of departure for many later works.

There is a real question of whether urban design after two decades has kept up with the boldest features of Marina City. While a latter-day Futurist group in Britain called Archigram was fantasizing in the 1960s about "plug-in" cities, Goldberg had actually built one, under the humble aegis of the International Union of Janitors. The union sponsored the project to bring people back to live in the central city, instead of fleeing to the suburbs where the janitors had no jobs.

Here, then, was a formula for revitalized urban life. Vertical "specialized" elements—not only the apartment towers, but a lower office slab flanking them—were plugged in by their elevators to a horizontal structure containing "generalized" services which the buildings above shared. At Marina City this structure took the form of a multi-level plinth, or podium lodged below street level, but not buried or windowless because it fronts generously on the river. If there were no river, the creation of a sunken garden adjacent to the plinth could provide light and air. This arrangement frees the traditional surface of the city for plazas or parks, or to be enriched by cultural or commercial recreation buildings such as the TV Studio/Theater at Marina City, with its slung roof.

One of the most striking anomalies at Marina City, however, is the surrender of what should have been a great pedestrian space to the automobile. Where Marina City might have had a landscaped plaza overlooking the river, bordered by restaurants and cafes, cars whiz across the open space to the helical garage ramps. These were the single touch of romantic technocracy the architect allowed himself in a design otherwise governed by humane purpose.

Goldberg several times returned to the Marina City *parti*, for instance in an unbuilt 1974 project for a colossal tower at Delaware and Seneca in Chicago, and in wild proposals for Denver and Detroit, where he would have looped roadways around triads of towers. In his best-reasoned works, however, he generally sought to put the automobile out of sight, where it belongs, most notably in a plan for the Affiliated Hospitals Center for Harvard Medical School in 1970. Unfortunately constructed only in fragments that lost the overall meaning, the health complex might have been the most brilliant of his vertical/horizontal combinations of towers. Here the towers contained facilities for internal medicine, maternity and pediatric care, neurology, and other separate medical specialties. These were lifted above a base that included laboratories, food preparation, laundries, X-ray departments, other general services, and parking.

Another influential lesson from Marina City was the lifting of the building on 17 levels of parking. This makes a certain kind of real estate sense, which in free-wheeling America may also be an architectural justification. The lowermost floors lack views and are therefore the least lucrative and hardest to rent. Consequently the lowest views at Marina City are 20 stories up, commanding a panorama of the entire city.

In an interesting design for Astor Tower in 1963, Goldberg dispensed with the first eight floors for the same reason. The base of the narrow shaft was simply left open, except for free-standing columns and an entrance lounge at the bottom of the exposed elevator core. The idea found an echo in Kevin Roche's project for a new Federal Reserve Building in downtown New York mounted on four corner columns 20 stories high, which in turn seems to have directly inspired Hugh Stubbins' Citicorp Building in midtown Manhattan.

Goldberg has probably never received due credit for his feats of structural brio, just as his delicious art nouveau decor of Maxim's, which he installed downstairs at Astor Tower, went pretty much unappreciated.

Yet what counts most in his architecture is the way his boundless social energy flows through the structures themselves. Technology softens, curving and recurving, with a clear natural ease as shells of concrete enclose spaces which Goldberg has shaped from clients' genuine needs, rather than from standardized notions of what buildings should be.

Hence the extraordinary crustacean forms, absolutely suited to practical use, which Goldberg developed in 1965 for the Menninger Foundation Clinic in Topeka, Kansas. Both mental patients and physicians, and not least nurses and other personnel, were given exquisite architectural consideration in the layout of consulting rooms, offices, and other private and public spaces. Equal care was accorded to actors and audience in another organic design, climbing a La Jolla hillside, for the San Diego Theater in 1969.

Granted, these unique commissions by their very nature cannot be prototypes, but Goldberg's method is the same for buildings with far-reaching applications. The Raymond Hilliard Public Housing of 1966, which replaced a hideous South Side slum, set a standard for low-cost, subsidized dwellings in Chicago which has never been surpassed. In contrast to the Soweto-like compounds to which bureaucrats, architectural and otherwise, consigned the poor, Goldberg understood from the first that people without money—both the elderly and families with young children—want *homes* like everyone else.

This led him to consider the interiors of individual dwellings, of how people really wished to live, with a sensitivity that was altogether rare in the design of public housing which in Chicago, as elsewhere, has been cranked out by the mile instead of lovingly crafted by the foot or the inch. Goldberg's refusal to settle for a pat solution was resisted by municipal and Federal bureaucracies. But he stood his ground and won. The result, he says with some pride, has been the premier public housing in Chicago, the only large project that has not been trashed or defaced, where no uniformed personnel are on duty. The cylindrical midrises for the elderly derive from Marina City, but the curvilinear vertical shells for families were a fresh invention, recalling sea creatures like the Menninger design but far broader in social impact.

To take a trip to the South Side with Goldberg, eating ribs, listening to jazz, might have caused some of his Astor Tower neighbors to drop dead of fright, but for me it was a revelation. We ran into a man at the Hilliard Housing who recognized the architect, and told him warmly: "You know our people. You know how to make good places to live." It was true.

Goldberg, virtually alone among prominent American architects, deciphered problems with highrise dwellings for poor families almost a generation ago with a penetration that was then matched, so far as I know, only by researchers in a few architectural schools, but characteristically, his solutions were less simplistic.

Unlike the professors at Berkeley, for example, who, with cause, argued for a "small is beautiful" approach, Goldberg, who feels that cities can be enriched rather than impoverished by high densities, has never accepted this idea.

In analyzing the need of a major corporation such as the American Broadcasting Company for an unbuilt project of 1963, Goldberg tackled a a prototypical problem on a still larger scale. He attacked the problem of ABC from the inside out. He found that the most important creative work among the 1400 headquarters employees occurred in "tiny segments of activity." The largest cluster of employees consisted of 85 persons in the accounting department; the next was

Raymond Hilliard Center, Cermack
Road and State Street, Chicago,
Illinois, 1966. Photo by Orlando R.
Cabanban.

Exterior corridor of Raymond Hilliard
Center. Photo by Hedrich Blessing.

Astor Tower Apartments, 1340 North
Astor, Chicago, Illinois, 1963. Photo
by Hedrich-Blessing.

the legal department with 30 people. All the other groups had 10 or less, including secretaries and support personnel. The organization lent itself admirably to small "modules" of space for offices, conference rooms, and groups of desks for teams working together. Goldberg thoughtfully arranged them on the periphery, surrounding "communal space" in the center of each floor, which surprisingly bore a distinct resemblance to community rooms in his circular Hilliard Housing for the elderly.

Not surprisingly, the optimum floor arrangement coincided with another "geocentric" plan—to use Goldberg's term for his cylindrical buildings circling a round core. This one would have been exceptionally slender and elegant, 60 stories high, undulating on the exterior to express the curving modular divisions within.

ABC in the strictest structural sense would have been a "tube," as pure a tube as bamboo. The walls would have been structural shells, taking vertical and lateral loads, and the plan would have provided 15% more in usable space, per square foot of construction, than a conventional post-and-beam building.

For ABC, Goldberg also invented an interior transportation system tailored to its specific requirements as a communications company, but probably applicable to many other corporations. There would be "express stops" for elevators on every fourth floor, and escalators between them would provide "local" service, closely knitting together the staff. Goldberg's meticulous analysis of ABC's corporate structure preceded by 15 or 20 years comparable investigations of spatial needs. Even today, only in isolated cases have such analyses become profound determinants of structural form.

But architecturally the glory of the design would have been the highest television tower in New York City. Far more dramatic than the now dismantled antenna which crowned Marina City before John Hancock and Sears eclipsed it in the skyline, ABC's tower—at once a gigantic advertisement and an amazing Constructivist sculpture—would have been a circular, open frame of steel, tapering at its foot and its 1200 foot summit, and braced at midpoint by the 60-story building itself. Unfortunately ABC eventually put up a nondescript box on the Avenue of the Americas.

Since then, using the same analytical techniques, Goldberg has also revolutionized hospital design in clustered geocentric forms, usually four circular "pods" combined in a midrise tower of eight to sixteen stories. The advantage of this arrangement is that all the capacity of a major health-care facility can serve small, subdivided areas in the pods, where floors in Goldberg's lexicon become "villages." The nursing stations at the core of each pod act as "village centers," minimizing walking distances, and making it convenient to observe patients—and not less important, for patients to see nurses, such that a rare sense of communal intimacy is established. To eliminate a crushing institutional mood has been Goldberg's chief contribution to hospital design, but the secret of this architectural kindness is the economy of space and structure which concentrates personal contact where it is most needed, between the quickly responding medical staff and patients needing help who no longer have to be unduly patient.

Although the distinction of these curvilinear hospitals is in their social design, their structural systems deserve notice in their own right as ingenious technical essays in the use of shell concrete.

Goldberg has never used shells merely as enclosures, or "coverings," as even so fine a structural artist as Felix Cendela has done. In his search for efficiency, Goldberg early realized—for example, in the softly luminous classrooms of the shell-roofed Joseph Brenneman School in Chicago—the economy of these structures, but the space within was what counted, and this made his "new shapes a friend rather than an enemy to new design."

Still, the world will always need squares as well as circles. Right angles made sense in the American urban grid. For example, in the Prentice Women's Hospital in Chicago the rectangular "support base" of the bed tower covers all the ground area available along the straight street frontage. This led to an inherent conflict between a rectilinear post-and-beam structure and the shell form of the tower. Where these systems had interpenetrated in previous projects, these structures did not coincide "cleanly," and disturbed interior traffic patterns.

These difficulties were not merely technical but aesthetic, and Goldberg resolved to minimize them in the Prentice Hospital. So he "invented"—his own word—a new structural shell form: a flowing concrete "stem" containing utilities, stairs, and elevators, which grew out of the base, then cantilevered outward, to merge with the vertical shells of the tower.

The transition between base and tower had great formal beauty, and would seem more handsome still if the buildings were taller, since they appear rather stubby. Goldberg therefore tried a different solution to the problem in the Good Samaritan Hospital in Phoenix, where the elegant bed towers were built directly on their foundations, and the surrounding base space was designed as a "collar," technically and aesthetically consistent with the whole concept.

The medical complex in Phoenix was also the catalyst of a renewal program in the blighted surrounding neighborhood, something Goldberg has not been able to accomplish in the Harvard hospitals because of bureaucratic ineptitude. But now his "villages" transmitted energy to a larger urban context, which he hoped for in all his larger projects, but had hitherto been mostly unable to achieve. One major exception was his health sciences megastructure at Stony Brook on Long Island, for the State University of New York, which he could rightly call a "medical city." With two million square feet of space in its multi-level base and the three bridge-connected towers gathering above—each tower different from the others because of its unique scientific and education role—Goldberg at last could put his theories into practice on a colossal scale. Stony Brook in some ways is his most fantastic excursion into the architecture of the future. It has the look of a NASA space settlement, but this health university is firmly grounded by its own road and communications system to serve 12,000 people daily. The "instant medical city" requires as much electrical energy as a small town. No less than one million cubic feet of fresh air has to be pumped into the complex environment every minute, and the air has to be protected from contamination. There are faculty and administrative offices, residences for students, libraries, labs, restaurants, computer banks, all kinds of mechanical systems which had evolved since Goldberg first devised a "total energy system"—utilizing heat from lighting apparatus—in the office building at Marina City.

By the 1980s it had all come together. Goldberg's inventions had been absorbed into the canons of biotechnical architecture without much acknowledgment from the planning and design professions. Because of the non-Miesian forms of his buildings, he was somewhat isolated from the Mies-dominated architectural establishment in Chicago, but he had known Mies before any of the local orthodox Miesians, and in many ways understood him better.

Besides, he had never relinquished the high Miesian principle of architecture as "an expression of its time," as inseparable from modern industrial civilization as Greek temples, Roman basilicas, and Gothic cathedrals had been from theirs.

And finally, in River City, he has the chance to affect the future course of Chicago by integrating his ideas in a curving megastructure half a mile long, sinuously following the river southward into the decayed industrial tundra of the old city of smoke and steel which is being replaced by the new city of microchips, services, social democracy.

Goldberg originally wished to build his most ambitious triad of towers at River City: mixed-use skyscrapers 72 stories tall, linked by sky-bridges, and containing everything from housing to schools and retail shopping centers. For complex reasons, and to Goldberg's regret, this Brobdignagian urban sculpture did not go ahead, but for me the less spectacular alternative that is being built will be more human, wandering along the water like a creature out of nature. It will provide a continuous variety of visual and social experiences as the building curves inward as the river flows into the boat harbor and then curves outward in diving terraces. It will house all kinds of shops, spas, exhibition spaces, parking beneath, and a richly varied population above.

Diversity within a rational structural order is still what Goldberg's architecture is all about. The different dimensions of the precast concrete panels permit a virtually limit-

*Prentice Women's Hospital Maternity
Center and Institute of Psychiatry of
Northwestern University, Chicago,
Illinois, 1974. Photo by Hedrich-
Blessing.*

*Proposed American Broadcasting
Company Office Building and broad-
casting studios, New York, 1963.
Photo by Hedrich-Blessing.*

*Health Sciences Center, State
University of New York, Stony Brook,
1978. Photo by Gil Amiaga.*

less variety of housing arrangements, from its top tier of penthouses to the apartments and townhouses below. Yet they show an overall harmony, enriched by planting, and by the interplay of light and shadow in the tall, undulating interior courts.

These spaces, made for the public at large, share a Piranesian grandeur, which, like the work of Goldberg generally, is everywhere built to the measure of man.

Allan Temko is the architectural critic for The San Francisco Chronicle.

Portrait of Bertrand Goldberg.

River City, Harrison and Wells Streets, Chicago, Illinois, 1985. Photo by Orlando R. Cabanban.

Atrium of River City. Photo by Orlando R. Cabanban.

List of Buildings by Bertrand Goldberg

1935
Higginson Residence, Chicago, Illinois

1936
Rear-Engine Automobile Project, Chicago, Illinois

1937
Orangerie, Grayslake, Illinois
Abrams Residence, Glencoe, Illinois
Mullins Residence, Evanston, Illinois
Prefabricated Plywood House, Lafayette, Indiana
Standard House, Melrose Park, Illinois
Ancell Residence, Kenilworth, Illinois
Toomin Residence, Chicago, Illinois
American Furniture Novelty Company, Chicago, Illinois

1938
Jacobs Residence, Glencoe, Illinois
North Pole Mobile Ice Cream Store, River Forest, Illinois
Clark/Maple Gasoline Service Station, Chicago, Illinois

1939
Wernicke Residence, Palos Park, Illinois
Furniture for Kirchheimer Residence, Chicago, Illinois
Katzin Residence, Chicago, Illinois
Heimbach Residence, Blue island, Illinois
Paris Residence, Highland Park, Illinois

1940
Standard House, Indian Head, Maryland

1942
Standard House, Suitland, Maryland

1941 and 1943
Standard House, Maywood, Illinois

1943
Mobile Penicillin Laboratory for Office of Strategic Service, Washington, D.C.

1946
Standard Fabrication Corporation Prefabricated Bathroom Units, Chicago, Illinois

1946-1952
Children's Built-In Furniture in Different Residential Projects

1947
Corporate Offices, Sheldon Corporation, Chicago, Illinois

1948
Calumet New Town (Project for General American Transportation Corporation) Calumet, Indiana
American Furniture Company, Chicago, Illinois

1950
Helstein Residence, Chicago, Illinois
H. F. Florsheim Kitchen, Chicago, Illinois
Paris Residence, Highland Park, Illinois
Measurement Corporation, Boonton, New Jersey

1951
Board Room for Pressed Steel Company, Chicago, Illinois

1952
Rush-Delaware Building, Chicago, Illinois
Unicel Prefabricated Freight Cars, Hegswich, Illinois
John Snyder Prefabricated House, Shelter Island, New York
Lillian Florsheim Residence, 1328 N. State Street, Chicago
North Kansas City Redevelopment Master Plan, Kansas City, Missouri

1953
Unishelter Prefabricated Housing Units, Hegwisch, Illinois

1954
Drexel Town and Garden Apartments, 48th Street and Drexel Blvd, Chicago, Illinois
Professional Arts Center, Highland Park, Illinois
*Chicago Last Department Store, Chicago, Illinois

1946-1952
Furniture Designs for Private Residences

1955
*Blacksher Garden Apartments, Government and Ethredge Streets, Mobile, Alabama
*Jannota Building, Chicago, Illinois
Woodstock Public Library, Woodstock, Illinois, 1955
*Arts & Building Center/Lighted Center, Chicago, Illinois
*Dearborn/Maple Apartments, S.E. Corner of Dearborn and Maple Streets, Chicago, Illinois
*Pan-Coastal Office Building, Mobile, Alabama

1956
Michael Todd's Cinestage Theatre, Chicago, Illinois
Al Warner Residence, Chicago, Illinois

1957
*Pineda Island Recreation Center, Mobile, Alabama
*Motel 66, Chicago, Illinois
Nashville Sewage Plant, Newport, Tennessee

1958
Flagler Marine Center and Civic Auditorium Master Plan, West Palm Beach, Florida

1959
*312-316 N. Randolph Building, Chicago, Illinois
Happy Medium Theatre, Chicago, Illinois

1960
Edelmann Company (Factory Addition), Chicago, Illinois

1962
Central Park Project Master Plan, Denver, Colorado
Marina City Detroit Master Plan, Detroit, Michigan
Marina City, 300 N. State Street, Chicago, Illinois
Joseph Brennemann Elementary School, Chicago, Illinois

1963
Astor Tower Apartments, 1340 N. Astor, Chicago, Illinois
*American Broadcasting Company Office Building and Broadcasting Studios, New York, New York
Edgewater Beach Hotel Banquet Hall, Chicago, Illinois

1964
Marina City TV Studio/Theatre Building, 300 N. State Street, Chicago, Illinois
John T. McCutcheon School, 4865 N. Sheridan Road, Chicago, Illinois

1965
*Menninger Foundation Clinic, Topeka, Kansas
*Beach Sky House, Boca Raton, Florida

1966
Raymond Hilliard Center (Housing), Cermak Road and State Street, Chicago, Illinois
Copley Plaza Master Plan, Boston, Massachusetts

1967
Boylestown Apartments, Boston, Massachusetts
Elgin State Hospital, Elgin, Illinois
West Palm Beach Auditorium, West Palm Beach, Florida
*Point Squanto Residence, Quincy, Massachusetts

1968
Health Sciences Center Master Plan, State University of New York, Stony Brook, New York
Eastco Warehouse, Westwood, Massachusetts

1969
*San Diego Theatre Project, La Jolla, California

1970
Centro Medico Docente Master Plan, La Trinidad, Caracas, Venezuela
Affiliated Hospitals Center Master Plan, Boston, Massachusetts
James Hoge Residence (Remodelling), Chicago, Illinois

1971
Stanford University Medical Campus Master Plan, Palo Alto, California

1972
Burns-Jackson Community Redevelopment Master Plan, Dayton, Ohio
St. Rose's Residence, Daughters of Charity, Milwaukee, Wisconsin

1973
Biological Sciences Research Building, State University of New York, Stony Brook, New York
Laboratory Furniture, State University of New York, Stony Brook, New York

1974
Prentice Women's Hospital Maternity Center and Institute of Psychiatry of Northwestern University, Chicago, Illinois
*Delaware-Seneca Bldg., Chicago, Illinois
Charles A. Dana Cancer Center, Boston, Massachusetts
Morgan Memorial Church of All Nations, Boston, Massachusetts
St. Joseph Hospital, Tacoma, Washington

1976
Health Sciences Center/Stage I Clinical Science Tower, Stony Brook, New York
Bayou Segnette New Community Development Master Plan, New Orleans, Louisiana
St. Mary's Hospital, 2320 N. Lake Drive, Milwaukee, Wisconsin

1977
Health Sciences Center/Stage II Basic Science Tower, Stony Brook, New York
*Walton Seneca Condominiums, Chicago, Illinois

1978
Health Sciences Center/ Stage II Patient Care Bed Tower, Stony Brook, New York

1979
*Nightworld Project, Orlando, Florida
University of Illinois Hospital, 1740 W. Taylor, Chicago, Illinois
Warren-Sherman Community Redevelopment Plan, Toledo, Ohio

*Park Place Condominium, Springfield, Illinois
*Harrison Center, Chicago, Illinois
Kasr el Aini Teaching Hospital Master Plan, University of Cairo, Cairo, Egypt
Proctor/Gardner Advertising Corporate Office, Chicago, Illinois

1980
River City I Master Plan, Chicago, Illinois
Clinton Elderly Housing, Boston, Massachusetts

1981
*Affiliated Hospitals Center Ambulatory II Building, Boston, Massachusetts
67th/Stony Island Redevelopment Master Plan, Chicago, Illinois
*Chicago Crystal Palace, Chicago, Illinois
WFLD Broadcasting Corporate Office Interior, Chicago, Illinois

1982
Metro Plaza Master Plan, Phoenix, Arizona
Good Samaritan Hospital, 1410 N. Third Street, Arizona
Brigham Women's Hospital, 75 Francis Street, Boston, Massachusetts
Hinsdale Office Park/Health Care Park Master Plan, Hinsdale, Illinois

1983
Hinsdale Hospital Addition/Renovation, Hinsdale, Illinois
Dardanelle Mid. School/Community Center, Little Rock, Arkansas

1984
Metro Plaza, Phase I Office Building, Phoenix, Arizona
Biosciences Research Building, Harvard Medical School, Boston, Massachusetts

1985
River City II/Phase I, Harrison and Wells Streets, Chicago, Illinois
St. Joseph Hospital Addition/Renovation, 2900 North Lake Shore Drive, Chicago, Illinois
Providence Hospital/Phase I, 1504 Springhill Avenue, Mobile, Alabama

*Indicates unbuilt project

WALTER NETSCH

by Albert Bush-Brown

It is not given to many architects, nor indeed to many in any profession, to achieve distinctive style, to benefit society through craftmanship, to be honored by both peers and clients, and to enjoy friendships with teachers, students, artists and leaders of political and cultural institutions; yet those extraordinary achievements (any one might suffice) are enjoyed by Walter A. Netsch, the architect born in Chicago in 1920 who carried some of America's weightiest architectural responsibilities for more than three decades as a General and Design Partner in Skidmore, Owings & Merrill.

A sensitive, thoughtful man whose brilliant intellect seeks meaning and order, Netsch early became fascinated with radio and electrical and mechanical functions, showed zeal for reading and research in disciplines relating science, people and environment, and set himself to study architecture at the Massachusetts Institute of Technology, where he received his Bachelor of Architecture degree in 1943. M.I.T. then was ambivalent about architectural directions. While a few young faculty members drew modern designs reflecting current Scandinavian architecture, the older and dominant professors continued the classical tradition of the Parisian Ecole des Beaux Arts and set their students grandiose projects such as a new university for the Middle East or a capitol for a New Republic. Such projects had at least two dividends: they forced first analysis of complex, unfamiliar conditions and then organization at a grand scale. When combined with M.I.T.'s structural and technical training, such analysis and organization provided a strong education, and Netsch, though ready even in 1943 to spring from any classical bonds, was an exemplary product of the best in M.I.T.'s analytic and organizing discipline, as Louis H. Sullivan, another Chicagoan at M.I.T., had been almost eighty years earlier. Any lingering classical or exuberant illusions were quickly chilled by Netsch's wartime

WALTER NETSCH

service in the Aleutian Islands as a member of the U.S. Army's Corps of Engineers, followed by membership in the hard-driving team that designed Oak Ridge, Tennessee, for the U.S. Atomic Energy Commission, which summoned Netsch's technical and organizational skills.

Although Netsch is through and through a Chicagoan, a realist and builder imbued with Chicago's heritage:—the pragmatism that John Dewey and Thornstein Veblen fostered and the artistic legacy of Louis Sullivan, John Welborn Root and Frank Lloyd Wright,—he started his architectural career in Oak Ridge, where he joined SOM in 1947. There began adeep and abiding personal association, Netsch's friendshipwith Nathaniel Owings, one of the firm's founding partners. Affectionately called "Nat,"Owings entertained great dreams for modern architecture in the United States. His enthusiasm excited even Federal and military clients, and given a good idea, Nat invariably swooped it into a still better and grander concept. That engaging quality, combined with enormous personal warmth, summoned young designers to a vibrant and willing team, with Netsch soon joined by the talented Edward C. Bassett. To them, Owings was a mentor,keeping purpose high, fending against internal and external opponents, and always encouraging professional growth including explorations that departed from the probable. To this day, Nat, who died in 1983, remains the conscience SOM is best admired for: architecture, not the firm, is what counts, and architecture at its noblest must be put in the service of powerful clients in government, industry and education who can affect great improvements for the populations of the nations's cities.

That dedication is visible in the U.S. Naval Postgraduate School at Monterey, California, which was Netsch's major project within Owings' office. Walking among the buildings erected in 1952-55, one is struck by the orderly plan, its fit of high and low rise buildings to form courts and vistas, and by the module of 18'8" column spacings for all buildings, whose fenestration is elegantly proportioned and accented at floor and ceiling lines by thin horizontal plates on reinforced concrete frames. Closer review reveals Netsch's analysis of program and organization of interior space to gather the science laboratories within a single multistory building, while electrical engineering, requiring flexibility, has a separate building, as do the Mechanical and Aeronautical Engineering Departments, which needed isolated, lofty, unobstructed spaces to house wind tunnels and pressure chambers. Remarkable too are the structure's dividends to cost reduction, meeting a Congressionally restricted budget of $15 a square foot, while giving the government a demonstration of admirable building.

Transferring to SOM's Chicago office in 1954 and elected a General Partner the following year, Netsch developed the concepts for two important office buildings. Although he would later gain fame principally for his universities, libraries and museums, Netsch applied his powerful programmatic and formal analysis to the first new construction the Loop had seen since the Great Depression. Built in 1956-58, the Inland Steel Headquarters Building at 30 West Monroe Street gave Chicago its first brilliant example of SOM's ability to design corporate office buildings on the same high level as their Lever House and Pepsi Cola Headquarters in New York. Still preserved in a model, Netsch's concept proposed a solution to three problems: gaining a strong vertical symbol on an important corner among classically piered and corniced buildings; obtaining open working floors with no columns for flexible offices; and gathering the vertical mechanical and electrical services together for horizontal delivery to the open floors. His concept was subsequently modified by Bruce Graham into the design that was actually built. In a studio on the north end of the building, Netsch conducted his architectural work for most of the next two decades.

Later, Netsch tackled the difficult problem of attaching a new structure to the existing Harris Trust and Savings Bank, also on West Monroe Street, which required ramped connections to match the new floor levels and was given a mid-building double-scaled plenum to shorten the delivery of services and free the top story for an executive dining room.

Increasingly, beginning in 1954, Netsch was absorbed by the new U.S. Air Force Academy at Colorado Springs, Colorado, which occupied his attention until 1962 when it was completed. The Air Force's choice of SOM evolved naturally from the firm's successful work at Oak Ridge, Monterey and airbases on Okinawa, but it was by no means sure, and each step in design development and public review required vigilant defense. There was first of all the entrenched taste of military officers, well known for keeping to the Gothic style at West Point and the Beaux Arts at Annapolis. Then there was the architectural profession itself who, if not opposed for traditionalist reasons, sometimes argued that so large a public commission should be assigned to several architectural firms. Then there were suppliers and assemblers of materials, especially the brick industry, who worried about the dominance of steel and glass. Overall loomed the great debate over how the beautiful foothills at the east face of the Rockies should be treated with native American architecture. Was SOM's design so servile to European architecture, especially to the style of Ludwig Mies van der Rohe, as to blaspheme that majestic setting? Frank Lloyd Wright said as much to a Congressional inquiry called by John E. Fogarty, member of Congress and lifetime member of the bricklayers' union. Now that the debate is stilled and the Academy is a generation old, the emotion

evoked in the 1950's is difficult to imagine. Congressman Hardy of Virginia thought the Academy resembled a cigarette factory. President Eisenhower is reported to have "flushed with anger" when he learned about the chapel proposed for the Academy, and it was widely supposed that he would have preferred the colossal classical Freedom Shrine he sponsored for the Potomac River shoreline in 1960.

What Netsch's design for the Air Force clearly declared was unmistakable. Architecture, it declared, has its own internal logic. Its form must follow that logic, without making imitations of agoras or forums or the ravines and peaks of regional landscapes. Like the Parthenon or Amiens Cathedral, the Academy should establish its own order, perfect it and let backdrop and vista enhance it. Until the Chapel provided the soaring vertical accent in 1960, the Academy was a stretch of horizontal buildings standing on mesas that had been graded to establish platforms for rectilinear buildings, each announcing a set of modular bays that are firmly incised with fine mullions and muntins framed by spandrels and columns. It is a brilliant display of precision, calibration and logic. The more public functions, around the Court of Honor on the uppermost level, are separated from the lower level, reserved for cadets' quarters, classrooms and dining hall, while the third or ground level is dedicated to vehicular traffic. The scale of courts and plazas was established to enhance cadet formation and group marching, and the orthogonal quarters and classroom buildings form walls and slots of space that define plazas. The one large enclosed space is in the Dining Hall, where 46 steel trusses support the 308-foot square roof. From the upper terrace, the Chapel rises like a faceted jewel, its seventeen glistening arrowhead points marking the aluminum clad tips of the internal tetrahedral structure, which is laced with stained glass. In one deft stroke, Netsch had created a unique symbol, one that clearly broke from the Miesian idiom and was exactly right for the Rockies' east face.

However prescient of Netsch's future, The Academy's Chapel seemed to be a happy sport, a brilliant but isolated idea without issue, without intimation of the profound departure from orthogonal order that was coming. Surely, the masterplan and buildings Netsch proposed for

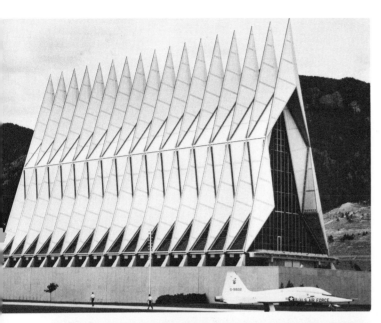

United States Air Force Academy
Chapel, Colorado Springs, Colorado,
1962.

Aerial view of United States Air Force
Academy, Colorado Springs, Colorado, 1962.

Art and Architecture Building,
University of Illinois at Chicago,
1965-1977.

Aerial View of the University of Illinois at Chicago, 1965-1977.

Behavioral Sciences Building, University of Illinois at Chicago, 1965-1977.

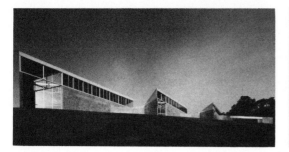

Louis Jefferson Long Library, Wells College, Aurora, New York, 1968.

Interior of Louis Jefferson Long Library, Wells College, Aurora, New York, 1968.

Art Museum, Miami University, Oxford, Ohio, 1978.

Interior of Art Museum, Miami University, Oxford, Ohio, 1978.

Center for Material Sciences and Engineering, Massachusetts Institute of Technology, Cambridge, Massachusetts, 1965.

the Circle Campus of the University of Illinois in Chicago in 1960 continued the analytical and organizational mode of Netsch's earlier form-making. Here, similar functions, such as lectures or laboratories, were gathered within buildings irrespective of departments. Functions requiring mass movement and interchange of students were assigned to low buildings closely clustered at the intersection of raised walkways. In the center, the learning centers within the lecture hall were technological models and the plaza on the roof above them is a concourse at the confluence of elevated granite walkways, with exedras and stepped seating as in Ancient Greek theater. The other buildings, especially the laboratories, are sober, meticulous renditions of rectilinear themes, not forgetting the literal display of structural attentuation in the 28-story administration building.

How surprising therefore to return to UICC in the late 1960's and come upon the Architecture and Art Laboratories, where prisms break forward from brick planes, voids cut into corners, and truncated pyramids rise from roofs. The interiors shape axial spaces that participate in higher and lower spaces, while multiple and distant skylights admit spots, shafts and wells of sunlight. Also not announced in the early plan for UICC is the Behavioral Sciences Building, where a rising set of terraces formed by octagons, triangles and right angles creates an intricate silhouette. Perhaps the clearest statement of Netsch's developing aesthetics appears in the Science and Engineering South Building, where twelve modular units gather to form a laboratory cluster, four of which are then grouped around a central distribution shaft. Then, at the peripheries, the spaces formed by rotating a superimposed square are assigned to offices and small laboratories. It is a triumphant organization of rich complexity—a programmatic building whose intricate spatial sequences, faceted forms, strong accents and asymmetrical balances mark the edges of an otherwise monumental campus.

Netsch's statement at UICC was no less than the development of a generative principle resulting in a geometry that simultaneously defines plan, structural support, integrated mechanical systems, circulation and enclosure, with all spaces formed by walls, roofs and floors. Starting a plan initially with superimposed rotated squares, Netsch selected mass or void from the points, diagonals and hexagons within the lattice or field. In the 1970's, computer graphics assisted his three-dimensional study, but Netsch's selection remained a plastic choice within increasingly elaborate lattices, such as chrysanthemum patterns. His Lindquist Center at the University of Iowa and his Art Museum for Miami University at Oxford, Ohio, are elemental presentations of the selected possibilities, mature abstractions derived from artistic choice among potential orders within a field. The new aesthetic was first publicly revealed in Netsch's 1968 Library for Wells College at Aurora, New York. Standing on a slope, the Library is a bridge with three levels connected by a pedestrian street rising from the first to the third level and affording exhibition spaces along the walk. In plan, four 42-foot squares are staggered and rotated on a subordinated pattern of squares and hexagons to form the core, while similar squares stand alone or in a pair to form the wings. The resulting space is a single experience, sheltered by an undulating roof that helps to define numerous nooks and reading rooms. That such a library appeared on a campus riddled with Georgian, Victorian and Southern Federalist pastiches is a tribute to the Wells College President, Louis Jefferson Long, who chose Walter Netsch and stood behind him.

Indeed, Netsch's embrace of client and institution explains much of his success in aesthetic innovation on college campuses. No doubt his discussions with President Howard Bowen and the building committee at Grinnell College when the Burling Library was built there in the late 1950's led not only to the subsequent commission for Grinnell's Student Forum but to a computer center, science laboratory, hospital and the Lindquist Center at the University of Iowa, where Bowen subsequently became President. Again, reflecting the trust they placed in Netsch, a series of presidents at M.I.T. retained him to design the master plan for the neglected north campus and a long series of classroom, laboratory and service buildings. His Center for Materials Science and Engineering, completed in 1965, remains to this day an exemplary modern addition to a classical setting. Similarly, a bond developed between Netsch and Northwestern University. For the Evanston campus Netsch completed the master plan in 1960, a computing center, sports center and dormitory in 1965, the Lindheimer Astronomical Research Center in 1968 and buildings for administration, biology, medicine, music and engineering—a series that ended only in 1980. At a presentation to a building committee, Netsch showed himself always ready to take a scheme apart, even in the middle of a meeting, and sketch a new one that incorporated the clients' objections or new conditions raised at the meeting. His thoughtfulness, restraint and inventiveness invited committees to participate, but the process towards function and order remained unmistakably his as he sought root principle in what was constant and what was variable among the generalities and idiosyncracies of a technically and aesthetically complex problem such as the Regenstein Library at the University of Chicago.

The trust lodged in Netsch by important colleges and universities was returned by his deep affection and generosity to those institutions and to teaching. He accepted a trusteeship at Rhode Island School of Design and taught there in late afternoons and evenings. He served on vital committees at M.I.T., especially those concerned with the visual arts and M.I.T.'s collections. All the leading and many of the nascent schools of architecture appointed him visiting professor and invited him to juries, and he was awarded honorary doctorates by Lawrence University, Miami University and Northwestern University. Such academic recognition went apace with growing recognition within his profession: the Reynolds Memorial Award (for the Air Force Academy Chapel) in 1964, two National AIA Honor Awards (one for the Art Institute of Chicago and one for his work at M.I.T.) He was elected a Fellow of the American Institute of Architects and was appointed to the Commission of Fine Arts in Washington, D.C., which guides the architectural improvement of the nation's capitol.

Within that recitation of friendships and awards, there is little indication of the profound developments within Netsch's personal and intellectual life. Their nature and persuasion can only be hinted at here, but, stated simply, Netsch's affiliation with SOM became no longer the single focus of his life, and that membership was pressed to recognize his new and expanding freedoms and allegiances, not always understood or relished. Surely, his currency with contemporary painting and sculpture, including the assembling of a large and eccentric collection, was a strong aesthetic resource, often introducing representations of pattern and of wit that he did not find in architecture alone. His residence at 1700 North Hudson Street is a gallery where one lives at its edges. Secondly, there was the profound and affectionate companionship brought by his marriage in 1963 to Dawn Clark Netsch, Professor of Law at Northwestern University and Democratic Senator to the Illinois State Legislature. Of the multiple enjoyments in that marriage, surely the shared zeal for political engagement stands high among the assets of intellect, humor and conviction. In the 1960's and '70's, Netsch allied himself with causes for justice and civil rights, sometimes, as during reelection campaigns for his Senator, causing him to wear so many buttons that his jackets, already strained by broad, bony shoulders, sagged out of shape. But affection and sympathy for people in need were fundamental in Netsch's character, and two important architectural commissions revealed not only his determination to put his talent to social benefit but also his ability to persuade his SOM partners that such dedication is essential. Approached by the black pastor of St. Matthew's Methodist Church in Chicago, Netsch worked closely with him and his parishioners to design a new church, develop black construction management, raise money by their own means, and build the church within budget. A different but equally complete commitment is reflected in the Winnebago Children's Home at Neillsville, Wisconsin, now called Sunburst Youth Homes. Meanwhile, Netsch's projects for housing, transportation and urban design showed similar social commitments at large scale. Of those his studies for Pruitt-Igoe in St. Louis, the Detroit Paired New Towns, and his work on the Baltimore Corridor and Newark New Town are important records of his social service.

Unfortunately, the hour of Netsch's greatest summation of talent and influence was accompanied by a time of adverse change. In 1973, the first of the oil shortages brought a halt to office and industrial building in America, and most of the public and private universities had completed their building programs. During that pause,

Core and Research Library, Northwestern University, Evanston, Illinois.

Model for University of Tizi-Ouzou, including an academic campus and two student housing communities, 1978.

Aerial View of Northwestern University Campus, Evanston, Illinois, 1960-1977.

Winnebago Children's Home, Neillsville, Wisconsin, 1971.

Interior of Netsch House, 1700 N. Hudson, Chicago, Illinois, 1974.

The School of the Art Institute, Chicago, Illinois, 1977.

SOM took its architects abroad, chiefly to North Africa and the Middle East. Netsch was retained by Algeria's Ministry of Education to design the University of Blida, a hospital for Blida, and the University of Tizi Ouzou. His comprehensive plans for those projects reveal his mature individual style adapted to regional conditions. For Netsch, it was often a time of weary travel, protracted foreign negotiation, frustrating deferrals or abandonments; the toll to Netsch's health was heavy, and because he had put his back and heart into everything he had ever done, they required restorative attention. Moreover, during much of the 70's, Netsch's individual exploration and the special cultural clients he served within SOM tended to isolate him from the mainstream of the partnership, who were much happier with business clients and colossal projects such as the John Hancock Building and the Sears Tower. For several years Netsch conducted his work in an atelier apart from the office in Inland Steel. Some of his more personal and poetic statements, such as Miami University's Art Museum, were made there. But perhaps the epitome of his urban architecture summarized all of his professional and cultural commitments: the new entrance and wings of the Art Institute of Chicago, together with its School of Art, the restored Stock Exchange Trading Room and the gardens and pools where Louis Sullivan's arch forms the gateway to the museum. In 1979, though he remained Som's design con-sultant until 1981, Netsch took early retirement from his General Partnership. Since 1979 he has completed the concept for a library at Sophia University in Tokyo, submitted a dramatic computer-drawn tower for the Chicago Tribune competition in 1980, and turned his talent to painting, while becoming increasingly active with the Commission of Fine Arts in Washington, various advisory boards in museums and universities, Mayor Washington's review committee for the 1992 World's Fair, and advisor to Chicago's Friends of the Park.

Over a professional lifetime of hard, intensive work against deadlines, budgets and conventions, Netsch had gained his own aesthetic development within a great architectural firm. It will ever be questioned whether the achievement might have arrived without the resources and opportunities of SOM, but it is equally to be debated whether, as various honors and awards attest, it may well have been among SOM's finest accomplishments. He had won international acclaim for his educational and institutional designs and changed the image of a university as it had not been changed since the nineteenth century, and he was revered as a teacher and colleague and friend to those who were intent upon advancing the nation's best environmental and social interests.

Walter Netsch, 1965, next to
"Untitled no. 6, 1983" by Al Held.

Albert Bush-Brown graduated as an architectural historian and educator. He received his B.A., M.F.A., and PhD. from Princeton University. In 1950 he was elected into the Society of Fellows at Harvard University. From 1965 to 1970 he served as a presidential appointee to the National Arts Council. Dr. Bush-Brown has taught at Massachussetts Institute of Technology, the Rhode Island School of Design, and the State University of New York at Buffalo. In 1971, he was appointed President of Long Island University, a position he held until June of 1985. He is the author of two books: *The Architecture of America* (with John E. Burchard), 1960; and *Skidmore, Owings and Merrill*, 1983. Currently Dr. Bush-Brown resides in New York City.

WALTER NETSCH

List of Buildings by Walter Netsch

Garden Apartments, 1947 Oak Ridge, Tennessee.
Sukiran, Machinato, *Kadena*, Master Plans, Housing, (U.S. Air Force), (U.S. Army), 1950-1952, Okinawa.

Elmdorf Air Force Hospital, 1952, Anchorage, Alaska.
Greyhound Service Garage, 1953, San Francisco, California.
Massachussetts Institute of Technology, Karl Taylor Compton Laboratories, 1954; Center for Materials Science and Engineering, 1965; Center for Advanced Engineering Study, 1967; Center for Space Research, 1967; Central Refrigeration Plant, 1967; Classrooms and Offices, 1967; North Campus Master Plan, 1968; Central Cooling Tower and Oil Storage Facilities, 1970; Central Cooling Tower Expansion, 1973; Electrical Engineering and Communications Research Laboratories, 1974; and Heating Plant Expansion, 1974, Cambridge, Massachussets.

Inland Steel (Concept only), 1954.
United States Naval Postgraduate School, Engineering School, 1955, Monterey, California.

Harris Trust and Savings, (First expansion), 1959.
Northwestern University, Master Plan, 1960; Lakefront Landfill Addition, 1962; Computing Center, 1965; Student Sports Center, 1965; Undergraduate Dormitory, 1965; Lindheimer Astronomical Research Center, 1967; Central Utilities Plant, 1968; Rebecca Crown Administration Center, 1968; Core and Research Library, 1969; Biological Sciences Building, 1970; Center for Communicative Disorders, 1972; Regenstein Music Building, 1977; and Seeley G. Mudd Science and Engineering Library, 1977, Evanston, Illinois.

United States Air Force Academy, Master Plan and Cadet Area including Chapel, Humanities and Science Building, Administration Building, Recreation Building, Fieldhouse and Gymnasium, Museum, Athletic Field, Parade and Maneuver Grounds, Housing and Dining Halls, and Medical Clinic, 1962; and Religious Center, 1980, Colorado Springs, Colorado.

Lake Forest Academy, Master Plan, Dormitory, Faculty Apartments, and Academic Building, 1964, Lake Forest, Illinois.

University of Illinois, Circle Campus, Master Plan and Phases I, II, III and IV; Master Plan Review, 1965-1977; and Sports/Assembly Pavilion, 1981, Chicago, Illinois.

Children's Services Building, Administration Office Building, 1967, Chicago, Illinois; Illinois State Bar Association, Office Building, 1967, Springfield, Illinois; John J. Madden Clinic, Mental Health Clinic, 1967, Maywood, Illinois; St. Matthews Methodist Church, 1967, Chicago, Illinois.

Wells College, Louis Jefferson Long Library, 1968; Music and Art Center Remodeling, 1974; and Phipps Hall Auditorium Remodeling, 1974, Aurora, New York.

Newark New Town - In Town, Development Plan, 1970, Newark, New Jersey.

University of Iowa, General Hospital Addition and Outpatient Facilities, Design, 1970; Basic Science Laboratory, 1972; Educational Research Computer Center and Office Building, 1972; Health Sciences Library, 1973; and Lindquist Center for Measurement - Phase II, 1980, Iowa City, Iowa.

Montgomery College, Feasibility Study, 1971; Classroom Buildings, 1975; Library Additions, 1977; Science Building, 1977; Science Building Remodeling, 1977; Student Commons and Additions, 1977; Physical Education Building, 1978; and Speech and Music Laboratories, 1980, Takoma Park, Maryland.

Winnebago Children's Home, 1971, Neillsville, Wisconsin; Monument Circle, Urban Design and Transportation Study, 1972, Indianapolis, Indiana.

Detroit Paired New Towns, Conceptual Planning and Urban Design, 1971, Detroit, Michigan.

The Art Institute of Chicago, Remodeling of Prints and Drawings Gallery, 1973; McKinlock Court Terrace Galleries, 1974; Centennial Expansion Program, 1977; School of Art, Restorations of Sullivan Arch and Trading Room from Old Stock Exchange Building, 1977, Chicago, Illinois.

Operation Breakthrough, Design of Industrialized Modular Housing System, Master Plan, 1973, Indianapolis, Indiana.

Poinciana New Town, Master Plan, 1973, Poinciana, Florida.
Pruitt-Igoe Redevelopment, 1973, St. Louis, Missouri.
Westinghouse Electric Corporation, Master Plan, Research Development Center and Site Development, 1973, Churchill Borough, Pennsylvania.

John Wesley Powell Federal Building, National Headquarters for U.S. Geological Survey, 1974, Reston, Virginia.

The Organization of American States, Feasibility Study and Remodeling Programs, 1974, Washington, D.C.

Dirab Park, Master Plan for Wild Animal Reservation and Recreation Center, 1975, Riyadh, Kingdom of Saudi Arabia.

William G. and Marie Selby Public Library, 1976, Sarasota, Florida.

Mayo Clinic, Community Medicine Facility, 1978, Rochester, Minnesota.

Miami University, Art Museum, 1978, Oxford, Ohio.
Rush-Presbyterian-St. Luke's Medical Center, Regenstein Eye Center, 1978, Chicago, Illinois.

Sophia University, Central Library, Design Only, 1979, Tokyo, Japan.

University of Chicago, John Crerar Library, Feasibility Study, 1979, and Remodeling of Mandel Hall, 1980, Chicago, Illinois.

Fort Wayne Museum of Art, 1980, Fort Wayne, Indiana.
Texas Christian University, Mary Couts Burnett Library, 1981, Fort Worth, Texas.

University of Annaba, Three Student Housing Communities, 1984, Annaba, Algeria.

University of Blida, Academic Campus, 1984; Three Student Housing Communities, 1984; and Teaching Hospital, 1986, Blida, Algeria.

University of Tizi-Ouzou, Academic Campus and Two Student Housing Communities, 1986, Tizi-Ouzou, Algeria.

HARRY WEESE

by Wolf Von Eckardt

"I am a loner," says Harry Weese with more pride than regret. He is also a passionate Chicagoan, a sailor, an engineer, a historic preservationist, an urban designer, the publisher of an architecture magazine, and an architect with an eclectic, inconsistent style and remarkably consistent convictions.

All of this is inextricably related. Weese is a loner in part because he is "much too honest," as a friend put it, in speaking his mind about both architecture and Chicago to join the groups and cliques that set architectural fashion or play the city's political games.

As a sailor who ventures far out into Lake Michigan on his 44-foot ketch "Cumulus," he gains an elating perspective on the Chicago skyline that keeps reinvigorating his passion for it. "A mile out, I no longer hear the sounds of the city," he says. "Five miles out, I get the grand panorama. Still further, due to the curvature of the earth, Lakeshore Drive disappears and the skyscrapers seem to be rising out of the water."

His respect for nature infuses his urban and architectural designs. His engineering skill keeps them inventive and simple. Structure tends to determine the appearance of his architecture, rather than the other way around. Whether we are consciously aware of it or not, it is instantly and reassuringly plain to the eye what makes Harry Weese's buildings stand up.

Being one of the few truly literate architects around, Weese has never believed that modern architecture is, or should be, revolutionary. He sees building the human habitat as a continuum and values important old buildings as much as new ones. He was one of the first architects of his iconoclastic generation to fight for the preservation and restoration of important buildings.

Preserving individual achievements of the past is not enough, however. Disrespectful surroundings or an overbearing, bullying new neighbor, can be as devastating as wrecking balls. What matters, what

HARRY WEESE

makes cities livable, is the *tout ensemble*, the environment created by a group of buildings, the urban design. Harry Weese excels at that.

His concern is the city, which he has often compared to a garden that constantly needs cultivating, pruning, reseeding, replanting. A garden consists of a great variety of plants; a city is eclectic.

A consistent style, then, would be inconsistent with his thinking. "If present day architecture is ever to mature, it needs to eschew the fashion of the moment and consider the realities of decades," Weese told architecture critic Paul Heyer two decades ago. "We are willing to risk seeming inconsistent. I get a great deal of pleasure in discovering new combinations."

Harry Mohr Weese was born in Evanston, Illinois, a suburb of Chicago, on June 30, 1915. With the exception of one year at Yale, he studied architecture and engineering at the Massachusetts Institute of Technology. Then, during the summer of 1937, bicycling some 1,200 miles through Europe, he studied towns and their buildings. "If you don't know everything that's been built in architecture, you shouldn't even draw a line," he once said.

On his return, he spent a year at the Cranbrook Academy of Arts near Bloomfield Hills, Michigan, which was then in its heyday. Thereafter, he went to work for Skidmore, Owings and Merrill's Chicago office. A year later, the country went to war, and Weese joined the Navy as an engineering officer on the same destroyer for 3½ years. Another brief stint at S.O.M. and, in 1947, he started his own firm.

Harry Weese & Associates is now a force of some hundred people in total, headquartered in Chicago in an ingeniously remodeled, romantic old timber warehouse near the Merchandise Mart and in branch offices in Washington, Miami and Los Angeles. It counts among the larger, as well as most important, firms in the country and is considered "young and energetic"— even daring. Harry Weese not only looks younger than his age; he acts younger.

In other architecture firms, one often wonders who does what; the quality and style of the design may depend on what young architect was hired last week. At Harry Weese & Associates, there is no question who does the designing.

"Designing!" exclaims one of Weese's friends. "You mean the fussing and fussing and still more fussing and sweating it out down to the last detail. Harry follows up on everything.

He is very much his own boss." And he produces very much of his own, individualistic architecture.

The wellspring of that architecture is Cranbrook, which seems now to be having a comeback under the leadership of Roy Slade, a painter and art educator.

Founded and designed in the mid-nineteen-twenties by the great Finnish architect Eliel Saarinen and his friends, Cranbrook is not an art academy so much as a small and select group of post-graduate workshops primarily concerned with the art of designing the hardware of civilization— from skyscrapers to teaspoons. Weese worked under Eliel Saarinen on city planning, but also dabbled in a variety of other crafts and spent enough time in the textile studio to weave material for a coat for himself. Among his Cranbrook fellows were his friend Eero Saarinen (Eliel's brilliant son and also an architect, who died in 1961), industrial designers Charles and Ray Eames, Niels Diffrient, Harry Bertoia and Florence Schust Knoll, and urban designers Edmund Bacon and Carl Feiss.

What with Saarinen *pere*'s often whimsical architecture and sculptor Carl Milles' frolicking bronze nymphs all about, the campus, combining an earthy sensuality with modern clarity, remains one of the country's most enchanting environments. Cranbrook design shows the influence of that environment.

Although Eero Saarinen's or Weese's buildings are certainly in the Modern mainstream (much as Eames and Bertoia chairs, Loja Saarinen and Marianne Strengell wall hangings, or Maija Grotell ceramics), they are not what I would call Orthodox Modern. Cranbrook is pragmatic. Orthodox, Bauhaus, International Style Modern, whatever the label, is ideological.

Orthodox Modern, however brilliantly and pleasingly, is forever expounding its modernity, its defiant and abrupt break with historic continuity. It is forever making "statements" about our new age of technology and the moral irrelevance of bourgeois values.

Cranbrook, guided by the passionate inventiveness and dry wit of Eliel Saarinen, set out to solve problems, which are, incidentally, the problems of this new age. But Cranbrook concerns are more down to earth—the prob-

lems a lounge chair poses to the human anatomy, the problems of long walks from the ticket counter to the gate in a large airport, the problem of building secure prisons without the humiliation of bars.

And in the end, Cranbrook has had at least as much influence on America's visual culture as the more widely known and propagandized Bauhaus. Cranbrook, wrote designer George Nelson recently, "is not so much a recollection of a nostalgic past as a suggestion that perhaps here is contemporary architecture before it was derailed by the technocrats."

Weese, along with Eero Saarinen, is probably the foremost exponent of this un-derailed contemporary architecture. "I am most strongly influenced by the Scandinavians," he says, meaning Alvar Aalto of Finland and Sven Markelius and Gunnar Asplund of Sweden, in addition to the Saarinens. Scandinavians tend to practice architecture as a practical craft rather than a cerebral art like Renaissance Italians or, lately and excessively, the so-called "postmodern" Americans.

Weese's Scandinavian affinity shows in his fondness for wood and brick— earth materials. A woodsy and early example is his Island Summer House at Muskoka, Ontario (1964), that combined under one copper roof a cave-like sense of shelter with wide-open views across the lake and into the woods. The First Baptist Church at Columbus, Indiana (1965) displays Weese's lyrical side. The sanctuary, chapel, community hall and Sunday school are composed into one expressive brick sculpture crowned by enormous, green slate roofs.

The 800-seat Arena Stage in Washington, D.C.,—an octagonal building housing a square stage—combines brick with reinforced concrete to similarly expressive effect. Built in 1962, the building is still striking in its fresh modernity, proving that expressing structure and following function still make exciting form.

Weese's Cranbrook or Scandinavian approach—as well as most of his early vocabulary, such as large expanses of brickwork and copper clad mansard roofs—has remained with him to this day. But no twentieth century architect can entirely escape the influence of either Mies van der Rohe or Charles-Edouard Jeanneret, who called himself Le Corbusier.

Island Summer House, Muskoka,
Ontario, Canada, 1964. Photograph by
Balthazar Korab.

First Baptist Church, Columbus,
Indi-ana, 1965. Photograph by
Balthazar Korab.

South Lower Campus, University of
Wisconsin, Madison, Wisconsin,
1970. Photograph by Balthazar Korab.

South Lower Campus, University of
Wisconsin, Madison, Wisconsin,
1970. Photograph by Balthazar Korab.

Arena Stage I, Washington, D.C.,
1962. Photograph by Balthazar Korab.

Middletown Municipal Building, Middletown, Ohio, 1976. Photograph by Hedrich-Blessing.

Campbell U.S. Courthouse Annex, Chicago, Illinois, 1975. Photograph by Hedrich-Blessing.

Time Life Building, Chicago, Illinois, 1970. Photograph by Balthazar Korab.

200 South Wacker Drive, Chicago, Illinois, 1981. Photograph by Hedrich-Blessing.

Harry Weese, 1975. Photograph by Arthur Siegal.

(Frank Lloyd Wright, for some reason, made little impression on him. "He somehow washed over me," Weese told Heyer. "I took him for granted and felt he took credit for the architecture of an entire area to which others contributed. He ran away from the city, and to an extent the great social dilemma of the Depression period.")

Even today, our architecture remains in creative tension between the classic and the romantic, Mies van der Rohe's bare, square Barcelona Pavilion of 1929, and Le Corbusier's expressionist, free form chapel at Ronchamps of 1950. Harry Weese's *oeuvre* often reflects this oscillating creativity.

He admits to leaning strongly towards Le Corbusier, although he must know that this French-Swiss genius is a Jekyll and Hyde figure, at once the chief villain and redeeming hero of what we have been building and destroying these past fifty years.

Le Corbusier, the villain, has devastated our cities with his simpleminded vision of "La Ville Radieuse"—a city of uniform skyscrapers lined up in a park along sunken freeways. There are no streets, no people, no life.

Le Corbusier, the hero, charged modern architecture with incredible vitality. "A building should return the space it takes from the earth," he has said, for instance, lifting his houses on stilts, or *pilotis*, to make room below them and putting playgrounds and gardens on their roofs. In contrast to the precise, geometric inclinations of German fellow architectural revolutionaries, Le Corbusier soon tired of Cubism and Constructivism and ventured wild, at times almost bizarre sculptural forms.

Weese's South Lower Campus of the University of Wisconsin at Madison, completed in 1970, has a strong, though restrained touch of Le Corbusier. It serves mostly art education with studios, art galleries, a concert hall. Slender columns, quite like *pilotis*, lift the building mass off the ground. Many different levels, spatial surprises around every corner and the interplay of vivid forms make this six-story complex somewhat of a giant sculpture. It seems to move.

Weese's Oak Park Village Hall, completed 1974, an inspired, functional monument to the civic spirit—a building of brick and timber—is pure Weese. It resembles nothing any other architect ever did. And yet the *audace* of the huge round windows, the temerity of breaking a corner out of the square building and twisting it around to open the interior court, would hardly have happened without Le Corbusier's trailblazing. The facade of Weese's Middletown (Ohio) Municipal Building, (1976) is more obviously inspired by Le Corbusier's sculptural facades at Chandigarh and elsewhere.

The eminent architecture historian Carl W. Condit credits Weese with being the founder of the heretical movement that broke away from Mies van der Rohe's dominant authority. True. But no one who was architecturally growing up in Chicago while the Miesian spirit filled the air could help inhaling some of it.

Consider Weese's Science Center at Beloit College, Wisconsin, completed in 1968. It is a complex of three brick buildings, unquestionably Miesian in their sparse, less-is-more classic lines, yet eminently Weesean in their sophisticated composition and detailing.

At the Time-Life Building in Chicago, completed two years later, Weese used not only Mies' seductive simplicity but also Miesian materials, steel and glass. At first glance, the building might be mistaken for a Mies original. At second glance, one remembers that Mies would never permit himself vivid colors by letting his corten steel rust or tinting his glass with gold. Color aside, it becomes quickly apparent that the wide bays and the rich, crisp details make the building decidedly un-Miesian, almost cheerful. Some scholars are additionally cheered by the thought that the building may be an updated reappearance of the first Chicago School, the metal frame architecture of William Le Baron Jenney, Louis Sullivan and Daniel Burnham.

More certain is that the Time-Life Building features the first appearance in America of the double-decker elevator. The upper cab of the elevator carries people to even-numbered floors while the lower cab takes them to odd-numbered floors. The invention reduces elevator shafts by thirty percent without decreasing service.

Similarly manifesting Weese's engineering ingenuity are the 60-foot-high columns that elevate the Mercantile Bank in Kansas City (1974). They manage to combine elegant slimness with fire safety (which usually requires a heavy masonry wrapping) because Weese filled them with a gravity circulating coolant, "a kind of antifreeze," he says.

Two of Weese's more recent buildings within the Loop have become noted Chicago landmarks. One is, of all things, a skyscraping prison. The other, equally surprising, a livable office building.

The prison is officially known as the Campbell U.S. Courthouse Annex, serving as one of the three of this country's metropolitan correctional detention centers. It is a 27-story triangular tower whose broad front resembles nothing so much as a giant, concrete version of one of those now obsolete IBM cards with narrow, oblong holes punched in.

The triangular plan increases the number of outside cabins, as it were, and decreases the need for drab, long corridors. The slits are window openings whose glass is only five inches wide. But Weese splayed the openings outward to give prisoners a better view. Stairwells and elevators are located in the corners. The roof holds a walled exercise yard. The site also contains an 850-car parking garage. The visual effect of the building is stunning.

The office building at 200 South Wacker Drive and along the east bank of the Chicago River also has an air of *jamais vu*. Its architectural novelty does not rely on the newly fashionable Neo-Art Deco glitter, but on its basic configuration: two triangular prisms, one shorter than the other, placed on a pedestal.

Pedestrians perceive the shape of the light gray aluminum and glass building as just one dramatic knife-edge wall. The building's social novelty is the recognition that office workers spend more time at their place of work than in their living rooms and are entitled, as members of an affluent society, to more than efficient drudgery. There is a landscaped riverfront and park, a marina, and a health club as well as the pleasures of a lofty lobby and a skylighted atrium on the top three floors of the lower prism.

If Weese has thus made life more bearable for a few hundred federal prisoners and work more agreeable for a few hundred office workers, he has, *mirabili dictu*, made riding the Washington subway positively enjoyable for millions of commuters and tourists.

Begun almost a decade ago and nearly completed, Metro, as the system is called, consists of a hundred mile rapid rail network that ties the two-and-a-half-million population Washington metropolitan area together. Aside from a chronically malfunctioning, bewildering and, even at best, consumer-hostile automatic magnetic ticketing or "farecard" device (a piece of high-tech machismo the authorities seemed unable to resist) the system is a model of efficiency. In ten years there has been (knock wood) no crime to speak of and, still more surprisingly, no vandalism. The trains are spic-and-span, handsome, quiet and fast.

But the greatest wonder is that the bureaucrats in charge selected one architect—Weese—to work as an equal with the engineers to make Metro handsome, as well as efficient. With the support of Washington's Fine Arts Commission, which kept looking over his shoulder, Weese chose to apply a uniform design theme for all the stations. They vary, not for variety's sake, but because topographic and engineering considerations call for such differences as the width and height of the tunnels.

The public is pleased. The *New York Times* put Metro first on the list of the less than obvious things for Washington tourists to see. "While seventeen million tourists a year gawk above ground at Washington's great stone monuments, memorials and seat of power" wrote *Times* correspondent Nan Robertson, "something amazing runs beneath their feet. It is the Metro, a subway system opened only nine years ago that is a superb marriage of form and function.

"Descend into its stations for an instant sense of noble, arching space and serene lighting. Not since the great railroad cathedrals of the turn of the century has American public transportation boasted such esthetic quality. Architects and engineers rate the Metro, designed by Chicago's Harry Weese, as among the great subways of the world ... It's enough to make any New York subway survivor sob with gratitude and envy."

Washington Metro, Farragut West
Station, Washington, D.C., 1977.

Proposal for Wolf Point Landings,
including the Fulton House (1981),
Chicago, Illinois, 1981.

Proposal for the development of 4,400
new boat slips using residuals from
the proposed 1992 World's Fair, 1985.

Model of Federal Triangle Building,
Federal Triangle Master Plan,
Washington, D.C., 1982.

Weese's other considerable contribution to the grandeur and livability of the nation's capital has not yet been realized. It is his plan for bringing life into the Federal Triangle, that forbidding maze of Beaux Arts government office buildings between White House and Capitol and downtown and Mall. It acts like a wall between the seventeen million tourists a year who visit the museums on the Mall and the downtown merchants who would dearly love to sell them goodies and refreshments.

Weese would turn a courtyard now filled with cars into an attractive walkway with outdoor cafes to lure tourists through the Triangle and provide for shops and entertainment on the ground floor of the office buildings to attract people after working hours.

The Federal Triangle plan is just one of many urban design plans—some implemented, some not—he has drawn up for parks, plazas, shopping malls, colleges, and entire new communities. He has worked from Cambridge, Massachusetts, to Palo Alto, California.

But Weese's true love, as noted, is Chicago. More importantly, Chicago would not be what it is without his scrappy devotion. His first big fight was early in the sixties when the Auditorium Building was threatened. Built in 1889, it was where Dankmar Adler and Louis Sullivan, the greatest American architects of their time, first proved their mettle. Weese convinced the powers that be that he could restore the badly neglected landmark for half the estimated cost. He did. And not only saved an important part of Chicago's glory, but also established the idea.

Daniel Burnham's Orchestra Hall (1905) and Field Museum of Natural History (1912) followed. There probably would no longer be a Navy Pier, Soldier's Field, or even the creaky old El to which the Loop owes its name and Chicago its soul, had Weese not given battle.

Weese's present preoccupation is with Wolf Point Landings, a six acre development along the Chicago River east of the North-Western Railroad embankment. It involves the conversion of a cold storage warehouse into condominium apartments, a grand marina as well as new apartment towers and waterfront retail. The idea is to bring people back into the city center to give it life and to exploit the great potential charm of the river.

But his great dream is to fulfill what in his magazine, the venerable *Inland Architect*, he called "Chicago's Manifest Destiny." The grand plan would dramatize and celebrate the gift of Lake Michigan to Chicago by cleaning up the traffic confusion in Grant Park, restoring, enhancing and completing Daniel Burnham's noble diagram and adding thousands of new marina slips.

Weese, like Burnham, the master planner of the "White City" at the World's Columbian Exposition at Chicago in 1893 and of Washington's monumental heart, makes no little plans.

Weese would, in Burnham's words, "make the lakefront a living thing, delighting man's eye and refreshing his spirit ... It should be made so alluring that it will become the fixed habit of the people to seek its restful presence at every opportunity." Just as Burnham's opportunity for making it happen was the 1893 Exposition, Weese hopes that a 1992 World's Fair designed on Burnham's principles will do it.

It may not. But as architect Laurence Booth put it, "You have the feeling that Harry will go on having fun, solving problems, building buildings, surprising us for a long time to come."

Wolf Von Eckardt is a writer and critic with a special interest in architectural, urban, and industrial design. He was design critic for Time *from 1981 to 1985 and before that, since 1961, architecture critic and editorial writer for the* Washington Post. *Von Eckardt has contributed to a number of magazines, among them the* New Republic, Harper's, Horizon, Saturday Review, New York, National Geographic Magazine, Travel & Leisure, The Architectural Digest, Architecture *and* Public Interest *His articles are included in several anthologies.*

List of Buildings by Harry Weese

1956
227 E. Walton Apartments, Chicago, Illinois
U.S. Consulate Staff Apartments, Accra, Ghana
Lillian Schmidt School, Columbus, Indiana

1958
United States Embassy, Accra, Ghana

1959
Pierce Tower, University of Chicago, 5514 South University,
Chicago, Illinois
Hyde Park Redevelopment, A & B, Chicago, Illinois

1961
Northside Junior High, Columbus, Indiana
Old Town Apartments, Eugenie Lane, Chicago, Illinois

Arena Stage, Washington, D.C.

1963
Jens Jensen School, 3030 West Harrison, Chicago, Illinois
St. Thomas Episcopal Church, Menasha, Wisconsin
Otter Creek Country Club, Columbus, Indiana
Reed College Library addition, Portland, Oregon
University of Wisconsin Master Plan, Madison, Wisconsin

Morton Arboretum, Lisle, Illinois
Island Summer House, Muskoka, Ontario

1965
First Baptist Church, Columbus, Indiana
IBM Office Building, Milwaukee, Wisconsin
Cornell College Commons, Mount Vernon, Iowa
Cornell College Men's Dormitory, Mount Vernon, Iowa
Cornell College Women's Dormitory, Mount Vernon, Iowa
Southwest Washington Master Plan, Washington, D.C.

1966
Reed College Commons, Portland, Oregon
Reed College Sports Center, Portland, Oregon
Joint Institute for Laboratory Astrophysics, University of
Colorado, Boulder, Colorado
Laboratory for Atmospheric & Space Physics, University of
Colorado, Boulder, Colorado
Drake University Dining Hall, Des Moines, Iowa
Drake University Men's Dormitory, Des Moines, Iowa
LR#14 Townhouses (Hyde Park), Kenwood at Kimbark,
Chicago, Illinois

1967
Orchestra Hall Renovation, 220 South Michigan Avenue,
Chicago, Illinois
Physics Building, University of Colorado, Boulder, Colorado
John Fewkes Tower, 200 North Wells Street, Chicago, Illinois
Auditorium Theatre, 70 East Congress Parkway, Chicago, Illinois
Field Museum of Natural History, Roosevelt Road and Lake Shore
Drive, Chicago, Illinois

1968
Beloit College Science Center, Beloit, Wisconsin
Cummins Engine Technical Center, Columbus, Indiana
Air India Housing, Bombay, India
Fort Lincoln Townhouses, Washington, D.C.
Rochester Institute of Technology Library, Rochester, New York
Grant Park Master Plan, Michigan Avenue, Chicago, Illinois

1969
Latin School of Chicago, 59 West North Avenue, Chicago, Illinois
17th Church of Christ, Scientist, 55 East Wacker Drive,
Chicago, Illinois
Lincoln Park Zoo Master Plan, 2200 North Cannon Drive,
Chicago, Illinois
Shadowcliff Summer House, Green Bay, Wisconsin
Lake Michigan College Master Plan, Benton Harbor, Michigan
Forest Park Community College, St. Louis, Missouri

1970
Elvehjem Museum, University of Wisconsin, Madison, Wisconsin
Bank Street College of Education, New York, New York
Milwaukee Center for the Performing Arts, Milwaukee, Wisconsin
Formica Building, Cincinnati, Ohio
Time-Life Building, 541 North Fairbanks Court, Chicago, Illinois
Vienna South Master Plan, Vienna, Austria

1971
Carleton College Fine Arts, Northfield, Minnesota
University of Illinois Education & Communications Bldg., 1040
West Harrison, Chicago, Illinois
University of Illinois Physical Education Building, 901 West
Roosevelt, Chicago, Illinois

1972
Given Institute of Pathobiology, Aspen, Colorado
Actors Theatre, Louisville, Kentucky
Drake University Fine Arts Building, Des Moines, Iowa
IBM Building, Endicott, New York
University of Illinois Levis Faculty Center, Urbana, Illinois
Newberry Library Master Plan, 60 West Walton, Chicago, Illinois
Kreeger Theatre - Arena Stage II, Washington, D.C.

1973
Crown Center Hotel, Kansas City, Missouri
SUNY Law & Jurisprudence Library, Amherst, New York
Lavatelli House, Aspen, Colorado
First National Bank of Dayton, Dayton, Ohio
180 North LaSalle Building, Chicago, Illinois

1974
Oak Park Village Hall, Oak Park, Illinois
John Knox Home, Norfolk, Virginia
Mercantile Bank Building, Kansas City, Missouri
Lake Village East, 4700 South Lake Park Avenue, Chicago,
Illinois
Pershing Square Master Plan, Kansas City, Missouri

1975
University of Massachusetts Library, Boston, Massachusetts
Olmsted Student Center, Drake University, Des Moines, Iowa
New Trier Gymnasium, Winnetka, Illinois
U.S. Courthouse Annex, 71 West Van Buren, Chicago, Illinois
AMOCO Credit Card Center, Des Moines, Iowa
Grace Street Elderly Housing, 635 West Grace, Chicago, Illinois
Williams College Sawyer Library, Williamstown, Massachusetts

1976
First National Bank of Albuquerque, Albuquerque, New Mexico
Southern Illinois University Medical School, Springfield, Illinois
Middletown Civic Center, Middletown, Ohio

1977
Terman Engineering, Stanford University, Palo Alto, California
Washington Metro, Washington, D.C.

1978
Marriott Hotel, 540 North Michigan Avenue, Chicago, Illinois

1979
Grand Rapids Civic Center, Grand Rapids, Michigan
Prairie Capital Convention Center, Springfield, Illinois
1100 Lake Shore Drive Apartments, Chicago, Illinois
Mayo Clinic Harwick Building, Rochester, Minnesota
Steelcase Showroom, Merchandise Mart, Chicago, Illinois
Euclid Place Master Plan, Oak Park, Illinois

1980
Dade County Transit, Miami, Florida
Northwest Industries, 233 South Wacker Drive, Chicago, Illinois
AMOCO Credit Card Center, Raleigh, North Carolina

1981
Neiman-Marcus, Oakbrook, Illinois
Brown-Forman, Louisville, Kentucky
Fulton House, 345 North Canal, Chicago, Illinois
200 South Wacker Drive, Chicago, Illinois
University of Chicago Court Theatre, 5535 South Ellis, Chicago,
Illinois

1982
Riyadh International Airport Community, Riyadh, Saudi Arabia
Union Underwear, Bowling Green, Kentucky
Federal Triangle Master Plan, Washington, D.C.
U.S. Customshouse Post Office Restoration, St. Louis, Missouri

1983
U.S. Embassy Housing, Tokyo, Japan
Carbondale Public Library, Carbondale, Illinois

1984
South Cove Marina, New Buffalo, Michigan
Southern California Rapid Transit, Los Angeles, California
Adams-Wabash Station Rehabilitation, Chicago Transit
Authority, Chicago, Illinois
411 E. Wisconsin Office Building, Milwaukee, Wisconsin
Illinois Center Hotel, East Wacker Drive and Columbus,
Chicago, Illinois
Campeau Criswell Master Plan, Dallas, Texas

by Stanley Tigerman

Goldberg, Netsch and Weese. Three architects. Three native Chicagoans swimming upstream; struggling against the current; detached from their origins by the spirit of an age. Collectively they represent the morality of their epoch as each in his own way has tried to make society aware of the dangers of simplistic modernist thought.

Goldberg, Netsch, and Weese represented pluralism and complexity at a time when the last thing in the world people wanted to hear about was complexity. Americans were trying to formulate a synthesis by which they could show off their newly found victory of World War II. That synthesis was fulfilled first by Mies van der Rohe, and then, in one great gulp, by his followers. Corporate America, speculative developers, and institutions seemed to be interested in a combination of the practical with the aesthetically believable—all apparently plausible within the construct of Mies' discipline which placed emphasis on clearly defined structure and careful detailing of the curtain wall. Goldberg, Netsch, and Weese each operated within that milieu at times; and yet the three were individualistic architects within the American tradition of idiosyncratic architecture. Not that any of them were particularly eccentric in and of themselves—certainly none is even vaguely like the others, either in personality or in the nature of their work. However, they represented a hyperindividualism connected with, for example, a Frank Lloyd Wright, rather than a collective spirit that the American culture emerging out of World War II could identify with and present as a face to the world.

Goldberg came to maturity with the development of Marina City; a complex of wonderfully urban structures clustered about, and featuring two highly visible, structurally inventive residential towers—the "corn cobs" of Marina City. Commercially and critically successful, they soon led to a series of educational and health care institutional projects featuring the same structural-spatial-social concepts. But they never really became the example that one might have thought they could have become—somehow, they seemed too personal and eccentric for the taste of a national architectural community more interested in the practical sensibilities of the right-angled modernist approach to buildings and cities.

On the other hand, Netsch rapidly moved away from his early Miesian simplicity and elegance to a mathematically derived system that came to be called "the new geometry" or "Field Theory"—with the chapel at the Air Force Academy. Based on the unending permutability of geometry, Netsch's predominantly educational buildings rotated their way onto many American college campuses; computer applications expanded his theories. Still, the search seemed too personal to attract other architects in those geometric directions.

But the surprising failure was Weese. Here was an architect who, one would think, came on the scene at just the right time. He was inventive, apparently flexible, clearly interested in "contextualism" and most importantly, espoused genuinely held beliefs in people. To him, the expressed structural frame of Mies seemed appropriate for corporate America, while the vernacular tradition was right for domestic architecture. His buildings were sometimes magnificently inspirational (Baptist Church, Columbus, Indiana), sometimes not so inspirational (Marriott Hotel, Chicago). But the times were against his becoming a role model. The hunt for a simplistic single collective architectural spirit precluded others from falling in line behind Weese with his pluralistic aesthetic views.

Certainly, if there is ever to be a culture that can be called Chicago-inspired, it is absurd to think that each successive generation is compelled to go it alone—or worse—to suffer from the conceit that uninspired, if independent, thought is the basis of every generation's production. It is clear that Chicago architecture in particular derives its strength from Goldberg, Netsch, and Weese. The unconscious influence of these three, not of product, but rather of morality, will be seen to have influenced the generation immediately following. Goldberg, Netsch, and Weese have, probably inadvertently, become father figures to the vast majority of Chicago architects at work in the 1980s. Without them there would never have been a "minority report" to the massive majority report of the neo-Miesians. It is clear to me that without their respective energies, indeed without their failures as well, a successive generation of diverse talent would not have had the motivation to band together to posit a "new Chicago spirit."

Stanley Tigerman is a partner in Tigerman Fugman McCurry, Architects and Professor of Architecture at the University of Illinois, Chicago.

CURRENT ARCHITECTS

Cynthia Weese and Paul Florian

Current architectural practice in Chicago is diverse. Chicago architects execute an unusually broad range of building types which differ in scale and aesthetic sensibility. The following selection of architecture by Chicago architects is a sampling of buildings begun or completed in the Chicago area since 1980. It encompasses a broad range of commercial, residential and civic structures.

Most Chicago buildings are built by Chicago architects. Architects from other parts of the country are rarely considered for important projects, a situation which has, until very recently, given Chicago architecture a cohesiveness of style and execution. Continued attention to detail and to ornament as integral to a building's structure remain hallmarks of Chicago architecture.

CURRENT ARCHITECTURE

A number of new directions are, however, apparent. The faceting of the highrise shaft is a reaction against the anonymity of the Miesian rectangle. The extension of the curtain wall to conceal the position of columns reflects a waning interest in structural expression. The use of vernacular forms and materials indicates an increasing concern for the contexts of site and region. The selection of buildings in this section also reflects the greater involvement of contemporary Chicago architects in the design of interior spaces and in the restoration of existing structures.

Cynthia Weese is a principal in the architectural firm of Weese Hickey Weese. Paul Florian is a principal in the architectural firm of Florian Wierzbowski.

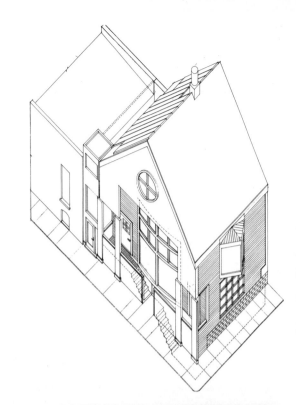

The Markle Building
Chicago

Architect: Ast & Dagdalen/Bruno Ast, Gunduz Dagdalen

Renovation of an existing frame structure into a single-family
townhouse. The architects employed both active and passive
solar systems.

211 East Ontario Building
Chicago

Architect: Barancik, Conte and Associates Inc.

Project Team: Richard Barancik, Erol Autay, David Kershner,
Ric Binalber

Photographer: Steven Arazmus

An eighteen-story urban office building of reinforced concrete
column and flat slab construction with aluminum panels.

O'Hare Atrium Office Center
Des Plaines, Illinois

Architect: Carol Ross Barney Architects Inc. (started as a
project of Orput Associates, Inc.)

Project Team: Carol Barney, Arthur Lytle, James Jankowski

Photographer: James Jankowski

Four-story suburban office building with central entry atrium.

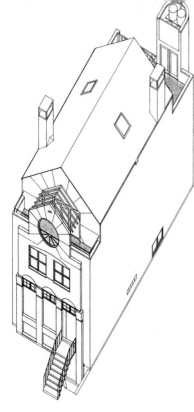

Simmons-Gill House
Lincoln Park
Chicago

Architect: Bauhs and Dring, Ltd.

New infill townhouse in historic neighborhood incorporating
materials and design elements found in the surrounding 100-
year-old buildings.

320 North Michigan Avenue
Chicago

Architect: Booth/Hansen & Associates

Photographer: Timothy Hursley, The Arkansas Office

A residential tower with an articulated top containing duplex
penthouses.

Mama Mia! Pasta
30 South Wacker Drive
Chicago

Architect: Banks/Eakin

Project Team: Garret Eakin, John Banks, Sui-Sheng Chang

Photographer: Orlando Cabanban

A fast-food Italian restaurant and bar.

Carrigan Residence
2057 Howe Street
Chicago

Architect: Stuart Cohen and Anders Nereim

Project Team: Stuart Cohen, Anders Nereim, Christopher
Rudolph, Terry Wiggers, Paul Griesemer

Photographer: Michael Goss

A complete renovation of a three-story post-Chicago fire townhouse. New spaces are elaborately trimmed with woodwork
reminiscent of that found in the original building; furnishings
were also designed by the architects.

Conrad Sulzer (Hild) Regional Library
4455 North Lincoln Avenue
Chicago

Architect: Joseph W. Casserly, City Architect Hammond Beeby
& Babka, Inc.

Project Architect: Tannys Langdon

A new regional library for the Chicago Public Library system to
house an eventual collection of 250,000 volumes. The second
floor is an open reading room with twenty-foot ceilings.

Restoration of the South Shore Country Club
71st and Yates Avenue
Chicago

Architect: Norman DeHaan Associates

Photographer: Chas McGrath

A complete renewal initiated by local community groups of a 1916
complex by architects Marshall and Fox. Interior colors and
finishes follow original specifications; the building incorporates
up-to-date mechanical and life safety systems.

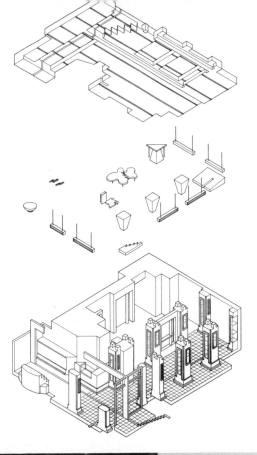

The Chicago Mercantile Exchange
10-30 South Wacker Drive
Chicago

Architect: Fujikawa Johnson and Associates

Project Team: Joseph Fujikawa, Gerald L. Johnson, Timothy
        Anderson

Photographer: Abby Sadin, Sadin-Schnair Photography

New trading floors for the Chicago Mercantile Exchange with
office space above. The top 38 floors of each tower are cantilevered over the trading floors to obtain required floor space.

Chiasso
13 West Chestnut
Chicago

Architect: Florian-Wierzbowski

Project Team: Paul Florian, Stephen Wierzbowski, Dan Marshall

Delineator: Michael Hennig

A store for designer housewares. Objects are displayed inside
columns of an arcade and on overscaled surrealistic objects.

Giordano's

Architect: Deborah Doyle

Photographer: Jeff Whyte

A prototype design for Giordano's pizza franchise.

St. Matthews Parish Center
Schaumburg, Illinois

Architect: Environ, Inc.

Project Team: John H. Nelson, Andrew Jaworski,
Ray Hartshorne, Terry van Dyne

A multi-purpose structure for religious functions and social
programs.

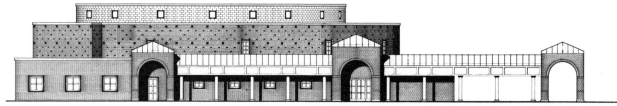

River City
Chicago River at Harrison Street
Chicago

Architect: Bertrand Goldberg Associates Inc.

Photographer: Orlando Cabanban

The first phase of a mixed-use development south of Chicago's
Loop, containing 446 residential units, office and commercial
space, a private park, and a 70-slip marina.

Mediatech Headquarters
110 West Hubbard Street
Chicago

Architect: HSW Ltd.

Project Team: George Hinds, Robert Nevel, Jan Czarniecki

The renovation of an early twentieth century warehouse into the
headquarters of a video production company.

Dearborn Street Station
Dearborn and Polk Streets
Chicago

Architect: Hasbrouck Hunderman Architects with Kaplan,
McLaughlin, Diaz

Restoration of a Chicago landmark into a shopping mall and
office center to anchor a neighborhood of converted lofts.

First Illinois Bank of Evanston
1900 Central Street
Evanston

Architect: David Haid Associates Architects

Photographer: Jim Hedrich, Hedrich-Blessing

Full service branch bank.

Beekman Place
Clark and Division Streets
Chicago

Architect: Gelick Foran Associates Ltd.

Project Team: Michael Gelick, John Clark, Joseph Bardusk

A multi-use complex merges 43 dwelling units with a retail and
office facility to complete an important urban intersection.

Catholic Order of Foresters Headquarters Building
Naperville, Illinois

Architect: Holabird and Root

Project Team: Jeffrey Case, Tom Welch, Tom Lassin

Photographer: Howard N. Kaplan

A U-shaped brick building with a free-standing colonnade which defines the entry court at the end of the drive and which extends on both sides to form sun screens for the south-facing windows.

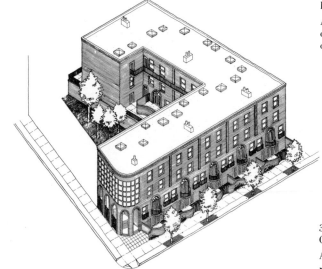

339 West Webster
Chicago

Architect: Gertrude Lempp Kerbis

Nine new multi-level townhouses in an historic post-fire
neighborhood.

840 Michigan Residences
Evanston, Illinois

Architect: David Hovey

Photographer: Bill Hedrich, Hedrich-Blessing

Twenty-four townhouses and penthouses around a central court
enlivened by high-tech detailing.

The Painted Apartment
Chicago

Architect: Krueck and Olsen

Photographer: Hedrich-Blessing

An apartment interior in a Mies van der Rohe building for a client
whose request was to live in a work of art.

Stanley Korshak
940 North Michigan Avenue
Chicago

Architects: Himmel/Bonner Associates

Project Team: Scott Himmel, Darcy Bonner, John Beidleman

Photographer: Barbara Karant, Karant Associates

A prestigious specialty store located within One Magnificent Mile.

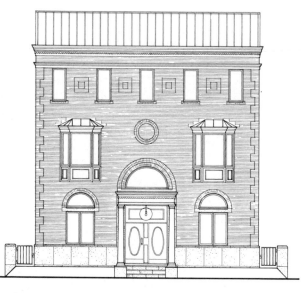

One Pierce Place for Trammel Crow Company
Itasca, Illinois

Architect: Loebl Schlossman & Hackl

Photographer: David Clifton

A fifteen-story investment office building with a four-story atrium lobby set in a 300-acre campus development.

1911 North Dayton
Chicago

Architect: Lisec & Biederman

Project Team: Michael Lisec, Fritz Biederman, Gregory Thomas

A new urban six flat with a facade designed to resemble a turn-of-the-century single-family house.

Miglan-Beitler Developments
200 West Madison Street
Chicago

Architect: The Landahl Group, Incorporated.

Project Team: Gregory Landahl, Jane Binkus, James K. Snavley, Lee Kreminski

Photographer: James Norris

Corporate headquarters for the developers of the 200 West Madison Building. The sawtooth glass partition echoes the exterior shape of the building and is sandblasted to simulate the exterior curtain wall in reverse.

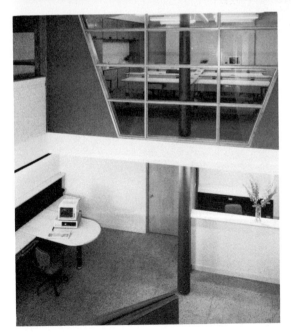

Triumvera Midrises
Glenview, Illinois

Architect: John Macsai & Associates Architects, Inc.

Project Team: John Macsai, Alfred J. Hidvegi

Photographer: Howard N. Kaplan

Six-story, sixty-unit apartment building that, together with
adjacent townhouses, form distinct residential clusters.

Young Artists Institute—Ravinia Festival
Highland Park, Illinois

Architect: Lubotsky Metter Worthington & Law, Ltd.

Project Team: Robert Lubotsky, James Law, Andrew Metter,
Wayne Worthington, Guillermo Cannon

Photographer: Andrew Metter

A year round music school on the grounds of the Ravinia
Festival. Included in the complex are a 450-seat auditorium,
practice rooms, music archives and offices.

PC & Micro Solutions Computer Showroom
Merchandise Mart   Chicago

Architect: Wm. McBride & Associates

Project Team: Wm. McBride and Jack Kelley

Photographer: Bones, Inc.

A bi-level facility incorporating sales, training, conference, and
office areas around a central two-story space.

North Western Terminal Project
Chicago

Architect: Murphy/Jahn

Photographer: Steinkamp/Palmer

A combined commuter terminal and office building complex to replace the former Chicago and Northwestern train station. The street arcade leads to a series of multi-story atriums experienced by both the commuter and office worker.

Addition to Lake Forest Home
Lake Forest, Illinois

Architect: Frederick Phillips and Associates

Photographer: Howard N. Kaplan

An informal living room addition to a single family house.

Mitchell's Jewelers
10 North Dunton Street
Arlington Heights, Illinois

Architect: Christopher Rudolph AIA

Project Team: William Sitton, William Allen, Thomas Radjovich

Photographer: John Hollis

Renovation of a two-story commercial office building. A new lime-stone and brick facade on the lower level replaces a 1950s aluminum storefront.

Winnetka House

Architect: Newman/Lustig, Ken Rogers, David LaPlaca, Al Fitzpatrick

Photographer: Sadin/Schnair

To insure privacy in a dense area, the house is formed around an inner courtyard which opens at one corner to permit an unobstructed view of the landscape.

Twenty North Michigan Avenue
Chicago

Architect: Nagle Hartray and Associates Ltd.

Project Team: Howard Kagan, Thomas Pociask, William Sitton, Mark Dilet, Victoria Seaver, Alexander Hartray.

Photographer: Hedrich-Blessing

Rehabilitation of a centrally located loft building and its re-use as retail and office space. A new central atrium provides light to interior office spaces.

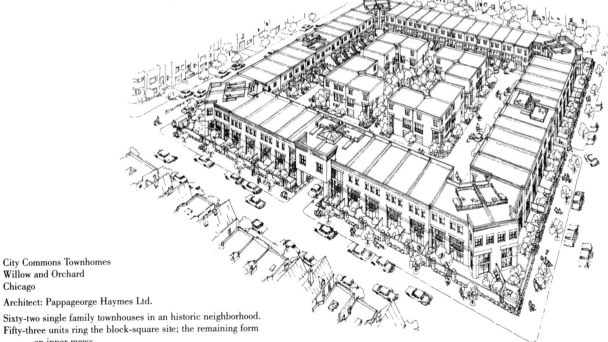

City Commons Townhomes
Willow and Orchard
Chicago

Architect: Pappageorge Haymes Ltd.

Sixty-two single family townhouses in an historic neighborhood. Fifty-three units ring the block-square site; the remaining form an inner mews.

Pre-School Space
Museum of Science and Industry
Chicago

Architect: Solomon/Dieckmann Architects

Project Architect: Richard Solomon

Photographer: Jim Steinkamp

A learning space for young children.

1418 North Lake Shore Drive
Chicago

Architect: Solomon, Cordwell, Buenz & Associates

Photographer: Howard N. Kaplan, HNK Architectural
          Photography

A narrow infill tower with one apartment on each floor. The
articulated facade preserves existing views from older buildings
          and provides panoramic views from each apartment.

123 Wacker Drive
Chicago

Architect: Perkins & Will

Project Architect: Ralph Johnson

Photographer: Orlando Cabanban

A high-rise office building which draws on traditional forms,
          particularly those of the Civic Opera House to the south.

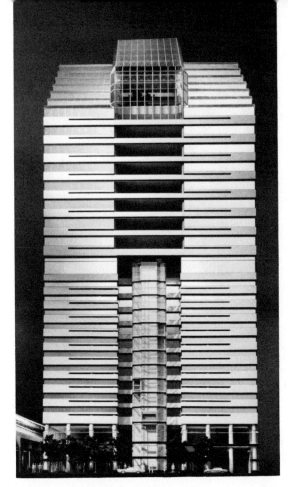

Loop Transportation Center
203 North Lasalle Street
Chicago, Illinois

Architect: Skidmore, Owings and Merrill

Project Team: Adrian D. Smith, Design Partner; Robert
Daimant, Partner-in-Charge; Peter G. Ellis, Studio Head.

Photographer: Orlando Cabanban

A multi-use structure designed to integrate a concentration of
transportation services with office and retail facilities.

Cobbler Square
1350 North Wells
Chicago

Architect: Kenneth Schroeder & Associates

Project Team: Kenneth Schroeder, Dennis Raffensperger, Drew
Raneiri, Jerry Guerts

Photographer: David Clifton

An urban conversion of the historic Dr. Scholl's factory and warehouse into a 297-unit rental apartment complex. New shops line
the street facade.

Skokie Valley Hospital
Skokie, Illinois

Architect: Schmidt, Garden & Erikson, Inc.

Project Team: R. Lange, D. Sagan, A. Kato

Photographer: Daniel Sagan

A five-story medical office building constructed of steel with a
pre-cast concrete skin.

Three Single-Family Residences
5748, -52, -56 South Kimbark
Chicago

Architect: David Swan/Architect

Photographer: David Swan

Located in Hyde Park, these three houses employ similar
volumes and motifs arranged to reflect different sizes and programmatic requirements.

Chicago Title & Trust Building
111 West Washington Street
Chicago

Architect: Jack Train Associates

Project Team: Jack D. Train, Mark D. Dewalt, Wayne F. Tjaden,
Kenneth D. Wertz, Michael Borowski, Jan Czarniecki, Brad Erdy,
    Lee Weintraub

Photographer: Nick Merrick, Hedrich-Blessing

A renovation of a D. H. Burnham building featuring a new two-
story central galleria with details and finishes characteristic of
    the era.

Weekend House
Lakeside, Michigan

Architect: Tigerman Fugman McCurry Architects

Project Team: Stanley Tigerman, Margaret McCurry

Photographer: Howard N. Kaplan

A retreat for two architects. The Midwestern forms of barn and
corncrib distinguish the screened dining porch from living, sleep-
    ing and work areas.

Single-Family Residence
Chicago

Architect: Marvin Ullman/Architects AIA, Ltd.

Project Team: Marvin Ullman, Henry Zimoch

Photographer: Wayne Cable

Complete interior renovation of an addition to a Victorian greystone. The interior open stair is placed diagonally in a skylit light well.

Suburban House Addition
Highland Park, Illinois

Architect: Terp Meyers Architects

Project Team: Lynn B. Meyers, Dana G. Terp

Photographer: Barbara Karant & Assoc.

A family room and master bedroom addition at the rear of a pre-World War I house. The architects designed the new rear facade to be similar to the front elevation of an old car—a humorous reference to the place a car usually occupies in the back yard.

Founders' Room
Field Museum of Natural History
Chicago

Architect: Office of John Vinci A.I.A.

Photographer: Tony Armour

Former executive office space converted into a formal reception area and conference center.

Phelan House
Winnetka, Illinois

Architect: Whitaker Associates

Project Team: Charles Moore, Donlyn Lyndon, William
Turnbull, Richard Whitaker

Photographer: Jessie Walker

A simple shed form under a single roof was manipulated both
internally and externally to meet the needs of a family.

The Bradford Exchange
Niles, Illinois

Architect: Weese Hickey Weese Architects Ltd.

Project Team: Tom Hickey, Randy Hafer, Rich Green

Photographer: Howard N. Kaplan

An addition to an existing office facility. Work spaces open into
a skylit garden with a waterfall; fiberglass tents shape the ceiling.

200 South Wacker Drive
Chicago

Architect: Harry Weese and Associates

Photographer: Hedrich-Blessing

An office building located at the edge of the Chicago river. The
size of the site and the angle of the river suggested the polygonal
configuration of the building.

Perhaps the best place to start in getting acquainted or enlarging an acquaintance with Chicago architecture is by calling the information number of the Chicago Architecture Foundation, 782-1776. A recorded message provides information about all of the tours run by the foundation as well as exhibitions, lectures and information on visiting the Glessner House by H. H. Richardson and the Widow Clarke House, both run by the foundation and located in the Prairie Avenue Historic District. The Foundation also maintains Archicenter, a useful orientation place in the Monadnock Building at 330 S. Dearborn Street where it is possible to buy most of the guidebooks and histories of Chicago architecture. The largest bookstore in Chicago dealing with books on architecture is the Prairie Avenue Book Store at 711 S. Dearborn Street.

Two organizations that deal with the preservation of Chicago's landmark buildings are the Landmarks Preservation Council of Illinois, 922-1742, a private organization devoted to the preservation of the state's important architecture and the Chicago Commission on Historic and Architectural Landmarks, 744-3200, the city's official body dealing with landmarks, the one that proposes landmark designations to City Council. Two major institutions that collect architectural drawings and mount shows on architecture are the Art Institute of Chicago at Michigan Avenue and Adams streets and the Chicago Historical Society at Clark Street and North Avenue. The American Institute of Architects, 663-4111, is a professional organization composed of registered architects, the Society of Architectural Historians, 1800 S. Prairie, a group of individuals interested in the history of architecture. Architectural schools in the city can be found at the Illinois Institute of Technology and the University of Illinois at Chicago.

Selected Bibliography

By far the best introduction to the history of the built environment in Chicago is Harold M. Mayer and Richard C. Wade's monumental *Chicago: Birth of a Metropolis*. This is one of the best urban histories that has been written for any American city and is a splendid way to get better acquainted with the city.

For a more purely architectural history the best place to start is with the books of Chicago's master historian of technology and urban history Carl Condit, his *Chicago School of Architecture, Chicago 1910-29: Building, Planning and Urban Technology* and *Chicago 1930-70: Building, Planning and Urban Technology*.

For touring Chicago's most important buildings there is *Chicago's Famous Buildings*, Third edition, edited by Ira Bach and his *Chicago on Foot*. In addition the Chicago Historical Society is putting out an excellent series of guides to the city. The first volume is already out under the title of *Chicago: A Historical Guide to the Neighborhoods, The Loop and South Side*.

GUIDE TO THE EXHIBITION

This section contains a floor plan and some of the highlights of the "150 Years of Chicago Architecture" exhibition presented at Chicago's Museum of Science and Industry from October 1, 1985 through January 15, 1986.

The exhibition–organized by Ante Glibota, director of the Paris Art Center–features more than 6,000 photographs and drawings, some 100 architectural models, pieces of historic Chicago structures, examples of construction materials, a typical architect's office, a multimedia show on Chicago architecture, and various educational programs.

The exhibit covers three floors totaling approximately 30,000 square feet in the Museum's West Pavilion:

ENTRANCE FLOOR: Most of this floor documents Chicago's architectural history, with special exhibit halls on the Chicago School of Architecture, Frank Lloyd Wright, Ludwig Mies van der Rohe, and the *Chicago Tribune* architectural competition. In addition, an orientation room, the multimedia presentation, and special historic exhibits can be found on the Entrance Floor.

BALCONY FLOOR: This floor looks at contemporary Chicago architecture. Ten prominent architects–including Bertrand Goldberg, Bruce Graham, Helmut Jahn, Walter Netsch, and Harry Weese–are profiled. The works of many other leading architects also are depicted. In two areas, various modern construction materials are displayed and explained.

GROUND FLOOR: A fully-equipped architect's office, a "hands-on" demonstration area, and exhibits dealing with world's fairs and architectural projects of the future can be found on the Ground Floor. A store containing architectural books, posters, and other materials is located at the exit.

The exhibition is the most comprehensive ever presented on Chicago architecture. More than 25% of the show has been updated and expanded since it began its international tour two years ago. It is presented in Chicago under the sponsorship of the *Chicago Tribune* and Carson Pirie Scott & Co.

Museum of Science and Industry

ENTRANCE FLOOR

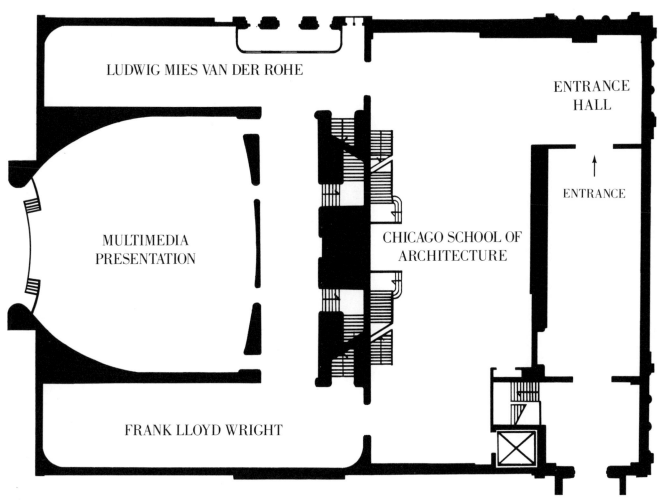

The Entrance Floor serves as an introduction to Chicago's architectural heritage. Among its principal components are the following:

ENTRANCE HALL: This orientation room looks at Chicago's present skyline and some of the early architectural masterpieces that have been demolished. The focal point is a section of the Home Insurance Building–the world's first skyscraper.

CHICAGO SCHOOL OF ARCHITECTURE: The importance of Chicago's innovative architects in the late 19th century– such as William Le Baron Jenny, Louis Sullivan, Daniel Burnham, and Dankmar Adler–is illustrated in this section.

FRANK LLOYD WRIGHT: The "Prairie" style of Frank Lloyd Wright sought to integrate design, function, and materials to achieve an organic harmony. Some of his original drawings are included in this hall.

LUDWIG MIES VAN DER ROHE: An exponent of the "Bauhaus" school, Mies van der Rohe believed that "less is more" in designing his functional glass and steel structures. His contributions are shown through photos, models, and furniture.

MULTIMEDIA PRESENTATION: The *Chicago Tribune* has produced a colorful multimedia show on Chicago's architecture. It is shown throughout the day in the Auditorium on this floor.

BALCONY FLOOR

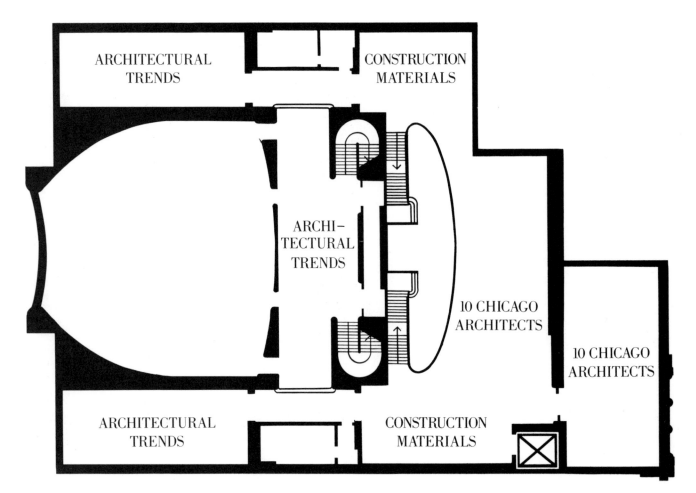

The Balcony Floor focuses on Chicago's contemporary architects and their multifaceted works. Highlights include:

10 CHICAGO ARCHITECTS: The contributions of 10 prominent architects are presented, including Thomas H. Beebe, Laurence O. Booth, Bertrand Goldberg, Bruce Graham, Gerald Horn, Helmut Jahn, Wojciech M. Madeyski, Walter A. Netsch, Stanley Tigerman, and Harry Weese.

SIGNIFICANT ARCHITECTURAL WORKS: Three halls are devoted to imaginative architectural developments from a design, engineering, and/or materials standpoint in recent years.

CONSTRUCTION MATERIALS: Examples of contemporary construction materials, such as steel, concrete, and glass, are displayed and explained on the north and south sides of the balconies.

GROUND FLOOR

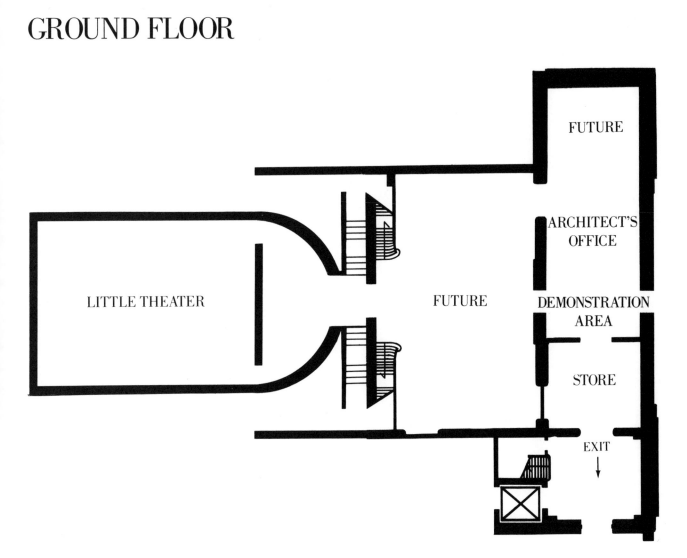

The Ground Floor looks at the future as well as the operations of an architectural office. The main elements are:

THE FUTURE: Various architectural and urban planning proposals and projects are exhibited, showing how the face of Chicago may change in the years ahead.

AN ARCHITECT'S OFFICE: A typical architect's office is presented and explained to visitors. The role of an architect also is illustrated.

DEMONSTRATION AREA: The public is invited to participate in "hands-on" architectural exhibits and to see live demonstrations.

ARCHITECTURAL STORE: Visitors may purchase architectural books, posters, and other materials in this well-stocked store at the exit of the exhibition.